Step-by-Step Podcasting for Business

Katharine Kerr

Podcast Pioneers 2021

CONTENTS OF THIS BOOK

OUTLINE

Introduction

- What is a podcast and why is it a powerful tool for businesses today.

Part 1 – Setting your course

- Is a podcast for you?
- Identifying your audience and the change you want to create
- Considering tone and presenter
- Time, energy and money
- Format
- Why explore the competition?
- What does success look like for you?
- Setting expectations and taking your colleagues on the journey

Part 2 – Designing your show

- What sort of treatments or 'formats' are achievable given the time and money available?
- How do I market my podcast?
- Release schedules
- Longevity and learning
- Having a Plan B
- Where to record?
- How to be useful to as many people as possible
- Branding sound and furniture
- Advertising your show

Part 3 – Producers, Software and Kit

- What a producer does
- When to invest and when to hire
- Getting started as a do-it-yourself podcaster
- Sound and kit basics

Part 4 – Show Preparation and Recording

- Structure
- Pre-planning interviews
- Editing for story
- The presenter's role
- Recording: How to prepare for anything

Part 5 – Hosting and Distribution

- RSS feeds
- Choosing a host provider
- How to set up, manage and distribute your podcast

Part 6 – Your Campaign and Strategy

- Integration
- What podcasting adds to your marketing
- Funnels and reservoirs
- 10 top tips to supporting podcast growth
- Getting the team on board
- Making a great trailer
-

Part 7 – Measuring Success

- What data is available
- Measuring the effectiveness of marketing channels
- Measuring calls to action in your podcast
- When to make a change
- Assessing your campaign

Foreword

Hello there and thanks for picking up this book. I hope it's going to be a useful and practical guide to get you started on the road to commissioning or producing a podcast from scratch. Whether you are a small business, corporation, NGO, charity or community project, audio can be a powerful way to share information, connect with people and issues, explore ideas, convey emotion and create change.

But audio is nothing without an audience. Audio is about creating a change and there are few ways more human, immediate and loaded with subtext than the human voice. Music and sound can move us and take us to other places. We can travel and be transported through audio and we can identify with different people through the tone or timbre of their voice.

Words and the spoken word, truly are the most democratising medium. It is no great surprise that self-publishing exploded once the technology became available.

To introduce myself, I am a former network radio producer from the UK. I left commercial radio in 2015 to pursue my passion for writing and journalistic storytelling, but couldn't quite leave my other love - audio - alone. And fortunately I didn't have to, because at this time a wonderful synchronicity was taking place in the UK audio world.

More and more people were beginning to listen to podcasts, which encouraged more and more companies, businesses and organisations to experiment with funding content in this medium as a way to connect with and grow their audiences.

I teamed up with my friend Neil Cowling at his company Fresh Air Production to help build a strategy that combined commercial radio programming concepts, and a strong sense of brand, with high-quality 'BBC-style' programme-making. Our first client was a British institution and household name. We held their hand through the pilots and today they have a dedicated in-house team publishing weekly content to thousands of passionate listeners.

Neil's production company was last year named Audio Production Company of the Year, having grown dramatically to a team of 15 producers (and it's still growing!). We still work together on projects that excite us, and I meanwhile, run Podcast Pioneers, my own audio production company that combines programme-making with integrated design, marketing strategy and asset creation for customers who want to incorporate podcasting with their wider communications channels.

This book incorporates many of the thoughts and lessons learnt in my time not only as an audio producer and writer, but as a commercial producer who works directly with clients from a wide range of sectors to communicate with their customers.

I also speak as a passionate audio and story-fan myself, as a curious human like yourself and a lifelong learner, like every podcast listener. For this reason, please excuse some moments of romanticism over the medium. It really does bring light to new places and podcasting, in my opinion, is one of modern technology's true success stories. Thanks to the medium we can reach across oceans and connect with people and experiences that are half a world away from our own. And more and more people are discovering audio in this format every day. Storytelling has become synonymous with the podcast format, playing upon memory, personal experience and emotion to absorb and stay with listeners long after they've moved onto the next part of their day.

Every idea is unique and every company different and so should your content be too. Every day podcasting becomes richer and more diverse and every day we learn more and innovate better in this evolving and fast-moving sector.

There are two factors that are quite unique to podcasting: the impressive length of time listeners are prepared to devote to an episode and the personal nature in which they are enjoyed. For any creator with an important message, this share of an audience's trust and emotion is precious.

This is not a book about how to monetise your podcast. This book aims to demystify the world of podcast production, and to help you build a successful strategy that incorporates audio content into your overall marketing plan. We will also explore how to best grow and market that content in the first place, so that it can deliver powerful engagement for your business.

I hope that the practical steps in this book inspire and inform you and provide a successful first step for you and your business into the wonderful world of sound.

Before we begin I would like to thank the friends and family who have read this book and made so many helpful suggestions in order that this book can make sense to people who don't necessarily speak the audio language! It is my hope that this is an accessible and practical read for people working in a wide range of sectors.

INTRODUCTION - WHAT IS A PODCAST?

Gone are the days when every conversation about a podcast had to include a discussion about what a podcast actually is. If you've picked up this book, the chances are you not only know what a podcast is, but you're curious and keen to know what this kind of content can do for your business and how you can implement it. That makes you the ideal reader of this book.

Many people know what a podcast is now, but enquire further and you'll discover that interpretations can be pretty diverse! Listeners often understand podcasts through how they use them. Whilst your understanding of what a podcast 'is' may be correct, you might also be missing what it 'can' be, and all that glorious potential.

That's because today podcasts can be radio shows, one-to-one conversations, events, documentaries, textbooks, gossip columns, self-help manuals, gripping dramas, stand-up comedy shows, guides to life and self-improvement. Plus so much more. In my opinion, podcasts are a medium through which one person engages with another person in a targeted and valuable manner, but which doesn't happen in isolation of all the other conversations those individuals might have. I'll explain that properly later though.

Perhaps you already know this and just want me to hurry up and get on with all the podcast secrets in this book. Well, even if your phone is packed to bursting with episodes you've downloaded and saved for later, even if your daily routine is filled with the sound of headphone chatter, it's absolutely worth acknowledging that some people don't listen to podcasts.

Actually, quite a few people don't. That might be because they don't know what a podcast is or don't have or understand the means of listening. In plenty of cases, they just don't understand what value investing reams of time in this medium will bring to their life.

For everyone else, podcasts are there for your enjoyment.

However, if you are the unique reader who has picked up this book without any prior conception of what a podcast is, then let's make sure we clear this up from the off.

A podcast is a digital audio file which can be made available to stream or download via the internet to your device. This might be a computer, phone, voice assistant or any web-connected player. The nature of that digital audio file - whether it's short, long, a one-off, a series, contains music, speech or sounds - is up to the creator.

The word podcast is used as a verb too, for example in 'to podcast a show'. The people who make podcasts are often called 'podcasters', 'creators', or more traditionally for audio programmes, 'producers'.

People sometimes ask if radio is the same as podcasting now, given that you can get your favourite radio shows, on demand. The answer is no. Podcasting is just the medium through which audio programmes are delivered, as is radio. The two mediums have different but complementary characteristics that allow them each to be of value to their audiences.

HOW DID WE GET TO THIS POINT THOUGH?

In their recognisable form, podcasts started to be developed around 2004, when radio shows and amateur audio blogs were becoming available online via devices such as the iPod. Many people hark back to Ben Hammersley's Guardian newspaper article where he asked the question: 'what do we call these programmes?' and suggested the term 'podcasting' alongside 'audio blogging' and 'guerrilla media'. We weren't yet at the point where people were using their mobile phones as audio devices or to surf the web. I still had a Nokia 3210 and accessed the internet via a series of cables, and then only when the moon was full and a South Westerly wind was blowing.

In 2005, Apple updated their player iTunes to incorporate podcasts and we were off to the races, with creators beginning to grapple with simple audio interfaces and software to record and edit their programmes.

By 2013, due to a combination of changing consumer attitudes to tech, better, more usable tech, and more mainstream adoption and awareness, podcasting was beginning to mean something to ordinary people. Comedian Rick Gervais was early to embrace and enjoy a successful, dedicated listenership, and in this year Apple announced 1 billion people had subscribed to listen to regular episodes.

It was still a strange place for businesses to dabble though, and the cliche of the nerdy guy with a passion for film or comedy prevailed. Businesses and organisations began to dip their toes in the medium, using it as another communications channel, and it certainly always has been a useful medium through which to share content with the visually-impaired, but here in the UK, there was perhaps little consideration given to the manner in which this could be presented. Step in the producers.

Radio stations were making their shows available 'on demand' as podcasts. Although in many cases their focus was in making radio than thinking about how on-air content could be repackaged or reinvented for people listening in a different way. At this time data on behaviour and demographics was a little sparse so measuring engagement or tailoring content to different needs was hard. But there was a growing community of audio experts who turned their experience and understanding of what makes a great show to this medium They began to experiment a make bespoke programmes. What's more, a few businesses and brands were willing to invest and explore this as another means of engaging with customers.

Plenty of people like to claim they were first to do this or that in podcasting, and there certainly were commercial and business-funded projects embracing or experimenting with the medium from early on. From my perspective though, I began to notice an upsurge in UK commercial podcast content around 2015 when I left format radio to look for opportunities in audio journalism and a different kind of content. It was hard to survive as a production company specialising soley in branded podcast content at that time but things happened quickly. With mainstream celebrities joining the movement, and an increasing acceptance by brands and influencers alike, the general public's curiosity and awareness of podcasting grew, as well as people's understanding of how it might complement their lifestyles.

Today, creating a podcast can be a powerful tool for your business, but there are several key things you need to know in order to make it a worthwhile investment. In my opinion now, it's high time businesses, organisations and commercial content creators took their audio output to the next level by incorporating this into their overarching marketing strategies and plans. This is something I passionately believe and founded my own company, Podcast Pioneers, to deliver. We need to do more than make beautiful things. We need beautiful, useful things that hold value for customers.

So with the basics now covered, I'm going to walk you through the thinking and approaches that I think are the secret ingredients to podcast success in business. This won't be a "how-to" for beginner audio editors and it won't be a book telling you to just hire an audio production company either. I hope to empower you to plan and make smart decisions about whether a podcast can work for your business and how to implement it for the ultimate goals: value, passion, advocation, promotion and awareness amongst your audience.

TURNING NEW AUDIENCES ON TO PODCASTS

In recent years, there's been huge growth in podcasting, thanks to increasing general knowledge around the medium. Advances in technology have made it easier and easier to create, distribute and access programmes. There's been increased provision by existing on-demand listening providers (such as music streaming services). Podcast apps are now built natively into default mobile phone software and we are seeing an increase in listening via in home voice-activated devices, which pairs well with audio and transcription incorporation into web search. Changes to the way we work and connect during the coronavirus pandemic has meant many spend more time behind screens just to get the day-to-day done, but podcasting offers respite for tired eyes too.

The future holds exciting possibilities for increased sophistication in the manner and ease with which we can access audio programmes online, from the development of AI and transcription services, as well as deeper analytic data for audience taste, demographic and behaviour.

This also raises some interesting moral questions around creative rights, privacy and data, which audio programmers, producers, distributors and commissioners are grappling with, and which you too must consider. The market has been very hungry and vibrant, which means a wealth of investment and innovation from the back to front end.

11

As a business, perhaps you have experienced the boom in podcasting with a grain of cynicism. There is so much content today, how can there possibly be enough demand? The podcast is here to stay, however. Audio programmes have for a long time delivered an essential and valuable service to the public. Whether it's in essential information, learning, entertainment or to augment the audience experience in some other way, the human voice is the oldest and arguably the most effective form of communication. Today, technology just enhances that, by conveying emotion, information and connection to people wherever they happen to be, whether it's in a crowded street, or alone up a mountain.

Most importantly: it's a personal choice to listen. And many people do.

As podcasting itself becomes ever more de riguer, people are cottoning on to the idea that it doesn't exist in isolation. Later in this book I'll talk about the value of building a robust marketing campaign around the medium, and how as a business you can maximise the impact and reach of your podcast by building it into your **network of communications**. (you might also hear this referred to as you digital ecosystem')

With any new technology, the theory is that you can follow its uptake in waves throughout time. First there are the early adopters, then eventually the mainstream. So to convert people to a new product over time, the user needs to:

1. Understand that the product can enhance and augment day to day life
2. Learn that's it's easy to use or access.
3. Crucially, begin to build a habit of use and access

Thanks to support in native listening environments such as radio, a larger number of audio fans have been able to experience the benefit of podcasts by understanding them as on-demand radio shows: the shows you love, whenever you want them. That's useful enough to show people the benefit. The other side of this is technology. Listening to podcasts requires your average listener to be mildly savvy with their listening devices - a phone or iPad or computer - for example. The global coronavirus pandemic certainly accelerated the digital transition for some mature demographics at a rate we may not have otherwise seen. Where necessity exists, or discomfort is high enough, technology really can present a solution, and as long as people are aware of the value of podcast content, there's an incentive for this medium to grow in every demographic.

Realistically though, when you start talking about apps or adding steps and hoops into the digital journey, you will start to see attrition to the number of people who can easily access your content. But there's still an audience, and when they've sought you out or discovered your podcast, the emotional investment is quite different to flicking on the radio stations and letting it do its thing.

As creatures of habit, **discovery i**s another challenge in converting non-listeners to listeners. Podcast listeners are hungry for entertainment and information, and once they find something they like, it's a case of hitting the subscribe button and knowing when to expect the next episode. Disappoint them at your peril: the moment you fail to deliver, their attention will settle upon something else, and you'd better hope you don't lose them forever! Fortunately, there is also a huge amount of loyalty in the figures. People invest a lot of one to one time in listening to their favourite podcasts - it's a special part of their day - a personal part.

On the other hand, listeners understand there is a wealth of choice in the medium, and our ever-moving minds are attuned to ever evolving stimuli, so there's opportunity to catch them at every juncture of decision-making and become their next great love.

Whereas your radio might stay tuned to the same channel for loyal listeners without much thought, when selecting a podcast to listen to a user is **actively** making a decision each time they listen. When you switch on your podcast app, you might continue listening to the same episode you left off on, and then after that roll onto the next, it's only ever going to be programmes you've selected. This experience is why radio and podcasting can co-exist: every diet demands variety. I'm loathe to describe radio as background listening, but it does tend to run under and alongside things moreso than podcasting, which I would suggest demands more regular attention and decision-making.

When your podcast listener opens their app, they can continue where they left off, go to their library of subscriptions, or, they can browse the library as they're used to doing with their on-demand TV platform every night. **This is an opportunity for you as the podcast creator, to get in front of them.**

Feelings happen faster than thoughts.

The decision, when made, might be based on **mood**, a problem they want to **solve**, something they are **curious** about, or **peer group** behaviour. They might also be more receptive because they've already heard about your podcast somewhere else, or seen your visual branding. Every choice our listener makes once they've fired up their podcast app has a driver, and this is your chance to give them what they're looking for. People are complex and unpredictable. So are their tastes, but it's your job to become a master of feeding them!

Serve your audience well, and they will return.

Also bear in mind that whatever episode they happen to play first is your opportunity to win them over, so every episode has to be just as good as the next. A quality product for a discerning, time-poor potential time-investor, is essential!

We'll spend more time exploring successful marketing in later chapters including advertising (above and below the line as part of the marketing mix). As this book aims to cater to those looking to create podcasts for their organisation's internal audiences as well as external audiences, I feel it's essential to frame our audio product in the realm of human behaviour, emotion and ability. I'm sure this will make a lot of sense to a marketer or copywriter, regardless of medium. If there's only one thing that you take away from this book, I will be sad, but I will very much hope it is this:

It's all about the audience.

The audience need comes first. If you focus on learning and serving these people, your content will be useful and that means emotional brownie points for your brand or business. With that in mind, let's get on with your podcast.

PART 1 - SETTING YOUR COURSE

In this section we'll tackle the questions you need to ask yourself before you begin:

- **Is a podcast for you?**
- **Identifying your audience and the change you want to create**
- **Considering tone and presenter**
- **Time, energy and money**
- **Format**
- **Why explore the competition?**
- **What does success look like for you?**
- **Setting expectations and taking your colleagues on the journey**

Your life will be easier, and your podcast campaign more successful, if you can ask yourself and your team some important questions up front. Step number one is setting the course for what success looks like, deciding who plays a role and establishing your style and means of getting there. Identifying your target audience is a question to be asked and answered from the outset. This can take hard work and commitment, so it's worth noting that a flaky strategy is likely to result in a flaky programme schedule and an unsuccessful campaign.

On the flip side, by bringing your team on board from the start and ensuring they are invested in the long-term goals to establish and grow a fantastically useful audio product, as well as positioning this correctly into the business marketing funnel, you will have the required adaptivity and buy-in to make this work long-term.

Making podcasts can be fun, but making successful podcasts can be fun AND challenging. This is the main difference between creating a podcast for your own enjoyment, and creating a podcast where investment, either of people's time, money or brand, is riding on it.

That's not to say that plenty of people haven't garnered success out of creating something for their own satisfaction. Indeed their personal investment is the thing that helps them keep going, even if it requires them to be ambivalent to the number of people listening. It may be the case these people have found a niche audience that loves their individual vibe. They might foster a connection with these passionate fans, grow a community and achieve the profile, longevity and reach that many define as success in the medium. But even star quality takes hard work!

Plenty of podcasters have run out of steam before they've even reached the first hurdle, and this is the risk you run if you embark on a podcast journey, hoping to achieve some sort of success for your business, without setting the waymarkers or destination. Especially if it's more than your own time and passion you're investing.

In this chapter we'll go through the questions you'll need to answer to inform your strategy, one by one, and explore why these things matter.

QUESTION 1: WHY DON'T WE HAVE A PODCAST?

Or rather, SHOULD you have a podcast?

Just because everybody else seems to be doing it, it doesn't mean you have to. By not asking this question, a company risks leaping gung-ho onto the bandwagon without considering whether anyone actually wants to hear from them in the manner they've chosen.

Often these attempts can be identified by an ailing podcast channel consisting of a smattering of rambling and barely updated interviews, released erratically, perhaps unedited, recorded variously in offices, on Skype or on the phone, with people likely only ever heard of within the company. It will undoubtedly be called something like The (Company Name) Podcast. There might also be a presenter (also internal) who's taken it upon themselves to play the role of raconteur Bruce Forsyth, even though their real life spirit animal is actually an accountant who likes jam sandwiches and silence.

Harsh, harsh, I know, and even this fictional example above might have some appeal to the people appearing on it. Sadly I've heard of cases where companies have paid an eye-watering amount of money to have this sort of thing 'produced' and distributed. Hopefully with the pointers in this book, you should be armed to avoid wasting your time and money in this way.

I should also add that it IS possible to record a fantastic podcast at your office, with your own staff. The difference is that the successful ones have considered all of these questions and used the answers to inform a strategy and editorial policy that subtly delivers the goods. In short, if you don't have an answer for these questions, you're probably not ready to invest your time and money in making digital audio.

But everyone can learn from their mistakes! When thinking about this first question, delve around and see if you or any of your colleagues or competitors have made any previous attempts at creating programmes for the business. How did they go down? How did you market them? How many people listened? What sort of responses did you get in terms of social shares, interactions or web hits? How does it sound and what's good or bad about the way it's put together? Anything you can learn from previous false starts or existing attempts will only be useful in thinking about what Your Amazing Podcast Mark 2 sounds like. Ultimately, leveraging any knowledge or experiences that exist within your organisation, good or bad, will be an asset.

QUESTION 2: WHO IS IT FOR?

The answer to this is your mission.

Clue: the answer is not Karly, the Head of Marketing, even if she put you up to the task.

As with any other digital communication, knowing who you will be talking to will influence your tone, style of delivery and the level of knowledge or experience you can assume when discussing your subject matter.

From now on, I'm going to start using the word 'audience' and 'customer' interchangeably. When you are making a podcast, you are creating a product, and whereas the person consuming it might not be the same as the person using one of your other products, having a clear picture of those people's needs and values is super important. Indeed, if you are already doing this across your product range, you may spy opportunities to market and bring in customers from your other products. It's all engagement with your brand, but the manner of it just differs from place to place.

Getting in the habit of always hearing conversations through your audience's ears is the role of anyone producing or presenting a podcast. Further to that, you should brief any guests on this before recording, and ensure that your presenter is clarifying, summarising and pushing to unpack key points as they crop up in the course of the show.

There are a few points to consider when honing your idea of audience. The 'average' podcast listener has evolved just as dramatically as the medium in recent years. In fact it's probably not that helpful to talk about averages any more, but we do have some statistics that will help build a picture of the kinds of people who listen.

The trope that early podcasters were predominately male, nerdy and relatively privileged was entailed by the fact that it required you to own the right kit, and to be engaged enough technically to use podcasting platforms. Back then, as a creator, you also needed the audacity to think people actually might want to listen to your brilliant theories on Star Wars.

Nowadays the access point, and price for listeners and creators alike is at a lower bar, and people have flooded to the medium as they enjoy its benefits. The subject matter is as broad as this new audience, too.

Some of the biggest podcasts are created by reality TV stars who still can't believe so many people are interested in what they have to say. And some of them are so clever they're barely accessible to human ears. There are podcasts designed to be listened to by the whole family in the car, or podcasts for mature audiences with very specific interests.

This presents incredible opportunities for innovation in the medium, and the style, content and nature of your programme goes hand in hand with understanding the audience you are creating it for. The beauty is that wherever your audience is, if you can identify their passions and market to them, you have an opportunity to get an almost undivided share of their attention and trust…. For some serious chunks of time. Anyone who's stood on a stage without their notes, or waited in the snow for a bus knows that that fifteen minutes can be a very long time.

How to identify your podcast audience

Your organisation probably has more than one audience. Speaking to everyone is a tall order. Think about where the passion and the potential lies. The first hurdle is talking to people in a space where they already feel comfortable.

- What are the main challenges or 'barriers to entry' for your audience? Is it time, laziness, misconception, lack of understanding or lack of awareness?
- What might help overcome these barriers? Where some of your customers spend their lives buried in their phones or iPads, others are only willing to give you their attention if you can help them balance a busy job with the demands of a domestic life and 2.4 children. Later we'll discuss how your marketing strategy can overcome some of the barriers above, and change perceptions gradually, so you can gather that long-dwelling, deeply engaged and loyal audience for your podcast.
- What are your audiences habits? Right place, right time has never been more essential. If you know your average customer already spends a great deal of time travelling, exercising or listening via headphones, then you're on pretty solid ground. Having this sort of insight allows you to design and market your podcast to the customer when they're at their most receptive.

Hard to Reach Audiences

When developing competition ideas for radio my colleague Liz's mantra was "Avoid too many hoops." i.e. keep it simple.

I love this phrase.

Why on earth would you ask your customer to jump through hoops in order to hear what you have to say? Are they going to do that, even for a chance cash prize, when they're already very busy? Often the answer is no. Never underestimate the strength of human inertia. We all have busy lives, and even when your best pal recommends a great-sounding podcast and you note down the name, you have to jump through the hoop of making time to search it out and listen.

If your listener has to add to that process the task of downloading an 'app' they don't understand, then please adjust your expectations.

If your audience is disinterested in technology, still uses the library to access internet and doesn't see why they need a mobile phone, then you might be barking up the wrong tree: You'd be better off buying a newspaper or TV ad or billboard outside their house.

If however, that audience regularly uses a desktop computer to check emails or their community Facebook page, or enjoys browsing the fashions on M&S.com via their household iPad, then you're in with a chance. Where there's an incentive for interesting content and your audience has the tools to hand, the chance to convert them exists.

What do we already know about podcast audiences?

This is where delving into existing company research will help you out - look at who is engaging with you on web, social or video channels and try to work out where you can increase the love with existing, digitally-engaged audiences.

Secondly, you may want to seek a new audience here. Perhaps you don't have much of a digital presence and it's something you'd like to grow. An audio strategy will be very much based upon the interests of your audience, so invite them in with some decent advertising in a place they are already engaging with you or your kind of service, the direct them to the podcast to deepen their engagement. This is obviously only going to work if you can convince them that your podcast is going to change their life for the better in some way.

A sidebar now, on the reasons why people listen to podcasts and how. We can safely assume listening is driven by any number of factors, from entertainment to education or information, because a friend recommended it, or because of peer group pressure and fear of missing out, to name a few.

There's some disparity between the various public surveys of podcast listeners in the UK, depending on who has commissioned the reports and what data sources they're using. This means that an understanding of your existing digitally-engaged audience, native to your other channels, is invaluable in making your plans.

However there are a few common factors across the board: Podcast-listening is largely a personal activity, and most people use their mobile phones to access them, followed by laptops and iPads and listen via headphones. As more people purchase and get used to voice-activated speakers in their homes, we might see a rise here, although the communal nature of these speakers makes them less suitable for niche content. The age range of podcast listeners has broadened out as the medium has become more mainstream. The 15-34 age category is largest, followed by 35-54. Expect that to level out more as people age with the medium.

By far the most convincing figure (should you be lobbying for internal budgets) is the massive engagement podcasts can deliver for their creators. The most conservative figure I've seen lately is that 65% of podcast listeners listen to the whole episode (Midas Spring 2020), and I've heard that go as high as 90%. Putting that in the context of the average episode duration (various sources put this between 20 and 40 minutes) and that is a long time to have someone's personal, full attention. It's a very convincing use of budget, especially if you add to this the support of an effectively deployed digital audience funnel, which will have ensured the listeners you do get are the really committed ones. I'll talk more about this in later chapters.

Because podcasts can be listened to any time, you might think that the time of day consumers are listening has no bearing on your product. However, if your content aims to set a certain tone or energy it may be worth bearing in mind: Peak listening dayparts are usually in the morning or journey home, much like radio really, this in mind might inform your tone and style. Although don't forget the little peak of lunchtime listeners, or bedtimers who like to drop off to something sweet. If you're going for this then it's all down to your marketing to make that appointment.

Think about what your chosen audience wants emotionally, and give it to them. You can then start to forge connections and become the provider of useful, valuable stuff. Quality is essential, of course. **If you can add value to a listener's life, you can add value to your brand or organisation in their eyes by proxy.**

QUESTION 3: WHAT CHANGE DO I WANT TO CREATE?

Or rather: how do I want my audiences to feel and behave?

"Just make them feel good about the brand": This is always a nice brief to be given as a producer - to just make something nice for this audience and leave them vaguely aware that so and so is the provider. If your organisation has a public-service remit, or wishes to be known for educating, communicating or supporting a certain endeavour or subject area, then all you have to do is make a show that people love, right? A GREAT show.

And you have to market it.
And grow it.
A tall order in itself.

It's always worth considering a deeper question at the brainstorm stage. If you are planning on doing the above, then why not think about what else you can achieve with the attention your audience are so kindly bestowing upon you?

The emotion you inspire is key: Loyalty to the podcast, and by proxy its publisher, is a good start. However, you might want to make them feel something about themselves. As a business, these are the feelings you'd want to stir up in your most engaged customers - these are the things your most loyal customers already feel about your products. What is it, and how can you do that in your content?

Perhaps you'd like them to feel clever or discerning. Perhaps you'd like them to feel welcomed to a community or special club. Perhaps you'd like them to feel like life is just a little easier with your business products around, podcast and all. Perhaps you just want them to join a conversation in your sphere.

Questions like this will help you when you have to come up with ideas for creative treatments.

The other half of this question is about concrete behaviour:

What happens when they've finished the episode? Do they just listen to the next?

What happens when they've finished the series? Do they just have to wait for the next?

What if you could keep the attention and loyalty of this listener and take it somewhere else? Even if you are an educator or public service, continuing to interact in this way is surely within your remit. You might then like to think about where you will direct your listener next, and how you might make them aware of this step via the fabric of your episode. What a great loss it would be to do all the work of getting someone to devote their time to visiting your podcast party, only for them to walk out of the door at the end and never come back, because there were no directions to the VIP area.

If you're selling a physical product or service and you want them to click and book, you could think about running ads during the course of your show, including special offer codes or having a little endorsement spot with your presenter. How you do this requires care, as you have an unspoken contract of intimacy with this listener, and they don't expect to be flogged to. Respecting their time investment in your podcast is vital to building and keeping trust and loyalty in your listeners.

If you'd like them to interact with your service or make an enquiry, perhaps you can create a webpage or social portal for this, and man it with podcast-passionate staff who will interact with the same, friendly tone as your audio channel.

If you'd like them sign-up for something, make sure the web or digital channel you direct them to also treats them like the VIP they became when they joined your podcast community, whether it's a mailing list with special offers, or discounted or free tickets to your events.

Maybe you just want them to listen to another episode or go to your website.

Ultimately, whatever your 'call to action', your listener / potential customer should be able to take their deep connection with your podcast channel to the next level and feel rewarded for it.

Worth thinking about isn't it.

QUESTION 4: WHO PRESENTS IT?

Why are you talking about this now, I hear you ask? We don't even have a format! The presenter has a vital role in catering to your audience, which is why I've suggested thinking about your options so early in the process. Your presenter is the shepherd that will invite, charm, direct and explain to your listener through the course of the episode. They'll ask the questions arising in your listener's mind, and push on the subject matter that intrigues them. They'll move things along when conversation drags, and they'll set the tone that's needed, whether levity, gravity, humour or flippancy are required.

The stars of TV and radio make this look easy, most of the time, but behind the curtain is the honed talent of a person who is intuitive both to their guests and their listeners. They must create rapport and trust within minutes. They are the conduit between the speaker and listener and it's their job to ask the questions that need to be answered, and draw out the tales that need to be told.

In addition to that, a natural curiosity and willingness to engage with the subject matter in a personal manner is key. And of course you need a good communicator; someone who can process and summarise content as they listen, who can adapt to and explore unexpected avenues, improvise, tread sensitively or push where it's needed, and who can steer things back to their intended course in time for the end of the interview.

If you weren't scratching your head already, the incredible ability to absorb and regurgitate reams of information at lightning speed is also a desirable quality.

Oh, and your audience needs to like them.

All of that said, some people are just born to do it. Sometimes first-timers pick up a microphone with all the right raw materials. The first episode is never that smooth, but before long their confidence and enjoyment grow as they get to grips with juggling all the inputs. On the other hand someone who feels uncomfortable in such a role may work hard to deliver, but fail to hide it. And they shouldn't have to. Not everyone wants to be in the spotlight and depending on the type of show you're making, it may or may not be necessary for your presenter to stand under it. There isn't just one kind of good presenter, and everyone has different strengths and weaknesses. The key thing is that your host cares about the project.

As a producer, you always breathe a sigh of relief when the person you've just met seems to have an earnest interest in the subject matter, so finding someone who communicates well and cares about the project will serve you much better than the office extrovert.

In summary, you don't have to decide on your presenter from the get-go, but having an idea of this would be helpful. whether you're looking at hiring A-grade TV talent, working with one of your celeb ambassadors, or picking someone internal.

QUESTION 5: HOW MUCH TIME DO I HAVE?

Looking for a quick hit? Overnight success? There are easier ways to make this happen than with podcasting.

An effective long-term podcast campaign gives its audience time to grow organically and build engagement across a back catalogue, in addition to the bursts of activity created by great marketing and advertising.

Your timeline should take into account not only the ability of your production team to deliver, but the capacity your supporting digital departments have to get behind the release and publishing of the programme. Your social media managers and all externally-focussed customer service staff will need to be ready to interact with audiences and take the content to the next level to build that loyalty. Success is not just about putting out a social post that commands 'listen to the podcast'. Even the most trusted household names can be guilty of this sort of promotion.

Depending on who you talk to, podcasters will say you need a good 3-6 months to start building a regular following so everyone involved in your campaign needs to be on the same page, from the moment you start promoting it, to release and beyond.

On another note, if the content you're creating is intended to be discovered and enjoyed at any time, then consider how older shows might be promotable at different times in relation to world or market events. This sort of content can create a "long-tail" of listening, where audiences coming in for the new stuff find great old stuff too, and thus the perceived value to them is immediately higher than if they were taking a chance on episode number 1, then waiting patiently for the next.

Obviously this doesn't apply to daily news shows and stuff that'll be out of date quickly. In those cases, supporting them with social and digital content that hooks into the current agenda and make them sharable and privately 'recommendable' as a daily habit is essential.

QUESTION 6: HOW MUCH BUDGET DO I HAVE?

Making great audio content can be remarkably cost-effective compared to some other mediums. But that's only half the story. Yes, you need a great producer to collaborate with, who has a track record you can hear and trust. But making the thing is only part of the journey. Making a podcast can be pretty straightforward. Provided you're not commissioning the world's most complex drama with a stellar casting line-up, the amount of energy, time or money you spend producing the programme is probably only about a third of the investment. The other two thirds go into promoting the programme.

You may already have digital and social teams within your business which means you already have resource to deliver a large chunk of that promotional spend internally. You can spread that figure over whatever your timeframe is, but it's there to manage your expectations: You may wish to do paid advertising or pay your presenter to do TV, radio or other podcast appearances. You may wish to create special video content, audiograms or host events. You may wish to run a competition on your website or hire specialists to work on the project.

I'm not saying you HAVE to do any of that, of course. You can still make a great programme and promote it yourself, but when you look at how it all adds up into a digital environment, investing more energy than you expect in promotion makes a lot of sense, especially if you are creating programmes that can exist in perpetuity, stay relevant and be listened to any time. You can re-promote your podcast any time there is something newsworthy to connect it to, or a surge in public interest for the topic.

Another good reason to spread your costs and think long-term.

Of course, having lots of great content will do a lot of the legwork for you once your first listeners start arriving, so creating an audio series versus a one-off will keep your reservoir of engagement fresh and prevent stagnation.

Set-Up Costs

Another thing you might wish to consider in budget conversations is whether or not you would like to hire-in consultants to help you get set up. If you are looking to invest in kit to record in-house, taking advice from producers and audio engineers who know their stuff will prevent you making costly mistakes. If you are not hiring a studio or will be giving an existing employee the task of recording your show, you may also wish to hire in training on how to best record sound in different environments.

QUESTION 7: WHAT'S MY TREATMENT?

Remember what I said earlier? **It's all about the audience.**

Hopefully answering the preceding questions will have begun to spark some ideas. It's always worth thinking big in the first instance. You can whittle down what's achievable once you've established your time and budget (so hopefully you worked through these questions in order!)

Maybe you've made a team effort, or each brought your own creations to the table. I'd urge you to be as adventurous as you like in imagining the best sort of audio show you could create. Forget for a moment, that you're a bank or a toothpaste factory or whatever, and think only about the calibre of programme that would have your chosen audience hooked - either on the edge of their seat in suspense, rolling on the floor laughing, or missing their stop on the train because it's so completely, damn absorbing.

Sometimes imagination needs a little help to get beyond its sphere of influence, so perhaps think about your favourite TV shows - not just radio and podcasts. What sort of formats and categories captivate your audience? Could it be a drama or a documentary? What about a hard-hitting investigation, or absurd panel show?
Is it interactive or educational?

Is there a cast of thousands or an empire of one?

Do you want to take them to places they've never visited, or immerse them in different experiences?

How could you harness user-generated content from your other digital channels to create content for this one?

What sort of amazing insight or unique knowledge and expertise do you have in your organisation, that might be of use to the wider world?

How will you tell the story?

What media are you audience already telling you they enjoy, that you may not have explored, personally?

What is the best thing you could sincerely and authentically want your most valued customer to receive from you?

How can you take a good idea and push it just a little further to achieve this?

The big splash

Another thing to consider at this point is marketability. If you've got a great idea, or a unique story, how will your idea or treatment become a catchy press-release that will create a buzz in other channels?

No true creator wants to be a copycat but it can happen! When I was a child my mother always told me to rise above it when other people copied my ideas and I've carried that through into my adult creative life somewhat obsessively! Always aiming for the moral high ground in creativity might mean you're prone to being hard on yourself, but on the other hand it can put you in a fantastic mindset for generating original ideas! My personal process for ideas generation is to come up with as many of my own as possible, before I check if its been done before. This means that you can silence your inner critic for a little while, pacifying it with the message that you will do a public sense check before things see the light of day. Also think as BIG as you can before you start chipping away with budget or time constraints. You can whittle your vision down to fit later on.

After that point, it's well worth having a look to see what your competitors are doing, and how you can avoid replicating that and just be better! How can you use the medium differently? How can you deliver something your competitors are not? And what is your Plan B if someone else pops their head up and gets in there before you? Competition is all good for making you work harder at this stage, but remember also that creating is not about trashing someone else, but improving on what is on offer for your customer. There are plenty of ears out there, after all! Some people even have two.

Educated intuition

However brilliant the concept and however high calibre the production, sometimes, bringing a fantastic show to market is a matter of good timing and good fortune. If you catch a wave on the rise, the same show might make a much bigger splash than one that was too early or too late. Listen to your audience and insights from you colleagues, examine the trends you're observing for your kind of idea, then head for the water when it feels right.

QUESTION 8: WHAT DOES SUCCESS LOOK LIKE?

By now you've worked out who you want to talk to. You've thought about what you'd like them to receive, how you'd like them to feel and what you'd like them to do.

You've come up with a killer idea and you're about to design the beast of all marketing plans.

So my final question before we get cracking is: how will you measure success?

If your goals for the programme are in audience behaviour, you may be looking to track click-through rates to a website using special URLS, then track their behaviour within your platform.

You might want to use your podcast - and someone else's - to deliver some host-read adverts or product placement. Special offer codes will allow you to see which show delivered different uptakes of the product.

Perhaps you want to do some general brand or subject matter education and have created a survey in order to measure how your listeners have absorbed specific messages.

Perhaps you are just looking to get as many listeners as possible.

Whereas you can design a programme to appeal to a certain kind of person, making sure it gets to as many of those people as possible requires you to use other tools to promote your content, so make sure you're not judging the success of your podcast on what is actually the success of your advertising strategy or audience funnel. Publishing content into an environment that contains 30 million episodes and expecting it to be an instant, magical hit is just not logical. It's like buying a lottery ticket and expecting to become a millionaire.

Whilst this is generally well understood now, not too long ago, selling podcasts to companies and brands was a little more difficult. Why? Because firstly, fewer people listened to them, secondly, their competitors weren't all doing one and thirdly, many businesses were used to buying audio on reach, as in, the number of people that theoretically listened to it.

If you're building a product from scratch, well, you don't have an existing listenership at all. My colleagues and I met this question by using marketing and advertising within channels where there was already a brand-engaged audience (more on that later), but ultimately the biggest spenders were those who, however corporate, didn't see the podcast format as an advertising medium as much as content marketing.

Podcasting is fantastic for measuring concentrated, self-selecting audiences who are highly-engaged with your brand, and this is crucial in what you expect to see from your audience: **They come giving you the benefit of the doubt and they stay because you give them value, intimacy, connection and a certain amount of consistency**. I suppose it's like dating really. Only once they know what they're getting and decide it's valuable to them, you just have to make sure you keep delivering, or offer ever more passion-invoking depths.

This isn't to say that you can't get some great listening numbers for your podcast to go with that epic listen-through rate (how long they listen before dropping off), but beware of promising your internal stakeholders something that ultimately will be decided by the effectiveness of your advertising and marketing. This is something it's always worth explicitly managing expectations for at the start of a project, if only to garner the support you need from other parts of the business.

That means involving and consulting social media teams, digital teams, brand, communications and marketing teams from the get-go, as everyone has a role to play in success, and hopefully a common benefit!

PART 2 - DESIGNING YOUR SHOW

In this section we're going to look in more detail at the following points:

- **What sort of treatments or 'formats' are achievable given the time and money available?**
- **How do I market my podcast?**

We'll also touch on:

- **Release schedules**
- **Longevity and learning**
- **Having a Plan B**
- **Where to record?**
- **How to be useful to as many people as possible**
- **Branding sound and furniture**
- **Advertising your show**

At last! The fun part! And if you thought this bit was going to be hard, here's the good news, you've already done the legwork. Answering all of those mind-bending, soul-searching, difficult questions will hopefully have worked you into a fever of ideas and conversation.

If not, then let's just recap your starting points:

1. Existing podcast attempts - what worked, what failed?
2. Identify your audience - don't be too broad.
3. Where do you envisage your audience fitting this podcast into their life?
4. Think about what value your podcast is adding to their life.
5. What do you want them to do or feel as a result of hearing your podcast?
6. Who looks like the best fit as a presenter? Do they have expertise in your area? How much briefing will they need to make your subject matter accessible to the audience.
7. How much time are you able to put into this on a regular basis?
8. How much budget can you set aside for production and promotion?
9. If you're investing in kit to record this in-house, have you set aside a budget for training and setup?

10. What does success look like for you and how are you going to measure this across other channels?
11. What timeline have you set to build your show, grow it and assess its impact on your business?

FINDING YOUR FORMAT

As you've listened around and done your research, you've probably realised that podcasts can be a lot more than the traditional, linear-style people at a desk interview. It's true that a large majority of programmes take this format due to its simplicity and relative affordability, but that's no reason for you to feel obliged!

We know that podcasts can go on physical journeys with listeners. Wherever their adventures take them, as long as their mobile phone is in their pocket, they can listen on commutes, supermarket runs, gym sessions, dog walks and long-haul flights.

But the opportunity to transport someone to another place via the power of their imagination has such a great allure too. As a writer, and someone whose previous career was in linear radio, I'm particularly passionate about getting your listeners to travel via a mobile medium like podcasting, even if they're just peeling spuds at home. I think even more of us producers should be harnessing the power of podcasting to take people places they've never travelled before, immersing them in sound and stimulus for a sensory adventure.

The very individual nature of imagination, based on someone's emotive, referential universe, means that the very same scene may look entirely different in one persons head to the next. In this way, audio is like a collaboration between producer and listener. You can give the cues, the clues, the sounds and the scene, but the real magic is in what their imagination does with it. It strikes me that there is so much more scope here to be personal than with visual mediums.

During recent Coronavirus restrictions, I had to re-plan and re-design location recordings that were scheduled over the early Summer 2020 period. This meant no gathering sound effects from castle ramparts or dungeons, no birdsong in an ancient wood, no rustling eucalyptus trees, no bustle of scientists or busy footsteps in the lab. But did we cancel our shows? No way!

Plenty of ongoing series were able to adapt to recording remotely via internet chats. After all, our mobile phones make for a pretty robust microphone backup at the best of times, even in highly variable recording environments. Whilst not as magical as the physical face to face, or location, in cases where customers were already recording in their offices or meeting rooms, not a lot was lost except the thrum of the centralised air conditioning systems. In fact, taking corporate recordings outside the office environment added a little informal je ne se quoit in some instances.

As for the big location pieces where space and place were key? We just adapted our mode of storytelling. By shifting our focus to description and objective storytelling in our interviews, and using stock sounds and music, we were able to reverse build a programme that sounds more like a fairytale than a sequence of interviews, ultimately dramatising the real. This still allowed us to achieve a sense of transportation, if not the very specific sounds of that environment.

So what about your format? Assuming you're working under less limited conditions than those induced by a pandemic, here are a few ideas with their relative pros and cons. Perhaps your ideal show will have a sprinkling of several different formats. There are no rules beyond delivering on the expectations you set for your listeners.

What's more, please don't think this is an exhaustive or definitive list of formats in any way. I'm sure you can dream up something wild and new if you want to!

Round table

Whether your "studio" is your garage, spare room, rehearsal space or a Skype chat from your respective kitchen tables, the round-table format consists of two or more people getting together to talk.

Pros -When it comes down to it, there's nothing like the humble human voice and unscripted conversation to convey emotion, intention and attention. We are masters at subtext in our own species, and the intimacy of the face-to-face environment, shepherded by a good presenter, can create the inviting and tell-all atmosphere so lauded in the medium. When comfortable and at ease in their own environment, a person might be willing to be more open and accommodating. Furthermore, hard to get people might be a little more willing to talk to you if this can take place in surroundings that they are familiar and comfortable with.

Cons -It's not the most original, is it? Add to that the variability in recording environments and getting your kit sounding good on location can be a fiddle without professionals, leading to a poorer sound quality and in turn, problems for the audience in hearing or immersing themselves in the conversation. Operator errors do happen, and so it's handy - and easy - to have a backup recording on your phone should anything go wrong.

Do it well by - Take care to do a decent edit on these conversations, even if it feels like 2 hours of magic when you walk out of the room. If you're in the room you might get wrapped up in the atmosphere and think someone's bathroom break was profound. A second pair of ears is advisable to make sure you're not boring or bombarding your audience with random information.

As for sound quality, plenty of people will say this doesn't matter that much, even professional radio presenters. But you probably won't ever hear anyone who's worked in sound engineering say that, because they're the ones working quietly and tirelessly to ensure that even poor recordings are to an acceptable standard. Execution may well not be as important as content, but if a poor sound distracts from the substance of a programme, or even makes your business sound homemade, doesn't it undermine the whole thing? With so many affordable, easy-to-use solutions out there and a vibrant market of experienced consultants able to offer advice, there's really no need to suffer with poor sound. Unless of course your producer forgot to press the record button, your SD card went wibbly or your cable froze and snapped.

Location-based

The atmosphere, spirit and sounds of a location, the sense of your cast of contributors responding to and describing real stimuli, the unexpected quirks that transport the listener away from that railway platform to another world.

Pros - The pros of location recording are numerous. Personally, I love to record on location and I'd hope through the power of writing I'm better able to set a scene for a listener as a result. Giving your presenters something physical to react to and describe is 1000% more enchanting to hear than having them interview someone else about it from afar. The immediate, personal and to some extent unpredictable nature of doing audio in this context makes it as exciting to make as it is to listen to!

Furthermore, if you get your sound recording and post-production just right, you can take people places they might never otherwise go. For example, I once designed a podcast audio tour around some well-known gardens, touching on the history, plants and sounds to capture the spirit. The thing I found most fulfilling about that project was the feedback from a listener who, when surveyed, said it made her feel she was walking around the garden. She was housebound with an illness.

I think the particular magic of audio is how you can create a scene through suggestion, with a little supporting sound to augment spirit and emotion, and the listener's mind does the rest of it. It's the ultimate collaboration of creator and listener imagination. It connects us, somehow. It's beautiful.

Cons - If you're on a windy hillside, or getting drenched by horizontal rain, it's tough. If you're walking around but you've not got the right kit and find your presenter is tripping over cables every 5 seconds, it can be stressful. I'm all for embracing the elements in a recording, but when your presenter has a runny nose, and your hands are seizing up from the cold, or your cables have frozen and cracked in sub-zero temperatures, the 'spirit' of the recording can be compromised. Don't get me wrong. I remember walking around the ruins of abbey one deserted, snow-capped morning, and the sound of the meltwater coming through the stones was unspeakably evocative. But my hands hurt so much I could hardly operate my recorder when my contributor arrived.

And if you don't have the right kit, it's not just the general mood of the production team that's dampened, but your whole sound. Plenty of times in my early experiments with wind, I had to just ditch the sound recording from the mix because my mic cover wasn't fluffy enough or my mic too sensitive in high winds. It's a real art to get this stuff right and there are people out there who specialise in it for a reason.

Once my friend Neil and I were planning to send a producer up Everest with an Olympian and a world-record breaking rower. Before we could even consider which kit to use, it was necessary to find a producer who was capable of 1) smiling in subzero temperatures 2) climbing and 3) not getting sick at altitude. As I dizzy on a warm Spring day didn't put my hand up for that one, but it was a useful research project and taught me a lot of respect for the people who are able to do this kind of thing!

Do it well by - Considering whether you need to bring in an expert to do your environmental recording. If conditions are more than a little atmospheric it will surely be worth it. Make sure you visit the recording site in advance and plan your recording locations and backup recording locations should you need to escape crowds, traffic or unexpected interruptions. Think about what sounds could complement your recording in advance, and give your presenter a chance to digest and feel into a place before you shove a microphone in front of them. First reactions can be quite fun to capture - the way someone interprets a place makes it really personal. Finally, some thorough research into the best kit is essential. This is hard because there is always more than one way of doing things, and many different opinions. It might be worth listening around for a programme that sounds great in such conditions and contacting the producer for some expert advice.

Unfolding Journey

Whether this is recorded on location or in the studio, this treatment allows you to knit your content together as a physical progression. Whether it's like the garden tour I mentioned earlier, or Foley-created sequences of narrative scenes, this is all in the storytelling.

Pros- It's immersive and escapist and allows you to make the most of the format, transporting your listener to another world and taking them somewhere with their own imagination. It's great for locations where there are multiple stories, contributors and angles to draw out.

Cons - You have to build a whole narrative to link one section to the next, and logistically you might not be able to record it all in sequence.

Also, if one of your locations is out of bounds on recording day, you might need to re-think how your narrative journey works without it i.e. the dungeon is flooded, there's a school group in for the day, high winds have closed some areas / the roads are closed etc.

Do it well by – Doing a reconnaissance to your location(s) first. Consider how you'll knit the places together. Is there value in the journey between one place and the next? Is this a place for your presenter's thoughts and reflections to emerge? Think about what sounds can you use to create space for reflection and a sense of moving forwards? And as always with location recording, have a backup plan in mind. Also, if you're doing a sequential journey in the final product, that doesn't mean you have to record it all in one day. Some space to think and swot up on research / back up your recording between locations is smart scheduling.

One-take sequence

You know on Saturday night TV when the presenter walks off stage and takes the mic with them, and the camera follows, and they go and surprise someone in their dressing room and do an interview in one shot? Wouldn't it be cool to play with something like that. Whether you're moving around your office on an audio tour, or taking a woodland walk and talking about the flora and fauna, this is a real-time adventure.

Pros - It's a nice gimmick: immersive, fully indulges in the flexibility of the medium and it feels somehow more intimate and behind the scenes for having no cuts.

Cons - Without an epic amount of planning, you risk including all the mundane, boring stuff that gets cut out of audio programmes for good reasons.

Do it well by - Planning it to a tee, and getting a great presenter who can react and improvise to situations as they happen with humour and warmth.

Documentary-Style

There's more than one way of doing a documentary of course, and how you build it is a creative choice.

You could research and gather all your audio first, knitting it together as a story afterwards, or you can storyboard it in advance based on your research and fill in the gaps as you go. You can knit distinct interviews or recordings together with analysis, context and archive audio, or you could take clips and smoosh them up next to each other to make a point. You could tell it from your personal perspective, revealing your thoughts and revelations as you go, or you could sit back as an omnipotent narrator and tell it all from start to end, already knowing, but not revealing, its course. Or you could take the 'explainer' out of the equation and let the listener fill in the gaps of understanding. As in all forms of storytelling, it's often the information you withhold that creates suspense, intrigue and questions. Are you going to present it all wrapped with a bow from the start, or get your listener do some thinking along the way?

Pros -You have massive creative flexibility with this format. Indeed, pretty much all of the formats we've described so far could be used in a documentary-style treatment. It's sort of a catch all term for telling a story and provoking thought and reflection in your listener around any kind of subject. Whether you want to inject suspense, surprise or provide a nice armchair account of some factual events from a well-balanced range of views, it's up to you.

Cons -If you like to have everything planned out in advance, you can be blinkered to surprises along the way. If however, you are happy to see where the story goes then great, but you risk not having any sort of coherent narrative if you're not analysing what's important and thinking about where it's going.

Do it well by - Keeping in mind where you want to go with the production, but never let your original plan for what you think the story is going to be stop it from taking a more interesting direction. That's not to say that you should go off down every little side-alley that presents itself and ditch the pitch, but if something unexpected happens to influence your story, such as an interview you never thought you'd get, or a candid piece of information that wasn't in your notes… well, you'd be mad not to adapt. After all, is it your job to tell the story or the story's job to tell itself?

When doing interviews with very knowledgeable, passionate people, I often come across interesting, but not directly-related stories that could be programmes or even series in themselves. It's always hard to leave them on the cutting room floor, so a bank of 'ideas to come back to' will help ease your conscience in the edit and allow you think about whether you'd like to return to them at the right time. Often I've ended up making bonus episodes out of these little side-notes.

Drama

The non-drama fan's preconception of radio drama might stretch to something theatrical; breathy, plummy, pathos-injected performances and soft kitchen-sink drama. I'm sure this preserve serves plenty, but it's not the only kind of drama out there.

2021 is the year of scripted podcast fiction. It's always been there, hiding out, but now the budgets are in plain sight, and that means big names and big writing as well as big exposure. This format isn't yet as deeply explored by the commercial world as others for a number of reasons: budgets can be high, and our ideas about audio drama in the UK are somewhat influenced by what we were used to hearing on national broadcasters in the past. Chatting to people who have a passion in this area, the feeling seems to be the same: there is a lot more to be explored in the drama space. The BBC is one of those in the vanguard, having in recent years made bids to break its own mould, with adventurous sound design and exciting new writers and commissions.

Still, the word 'drama' still feels a little loaded... a little.... radio. So let's talk about scripted audio fiction and scripted narrative instead.

Scripted Audio Fiction / Scripted Narrative

Whether you're looking at fiction or non-fiction, take a leaf out of the fiction-writers book - seek your narrative and themes and build them into story arcs for your characters. Think about point of view and how you can create suspense with what bits of story you hold back.

You might want to dramatise a true story with actors, or narrate a fictional one. The choices you make around point of view and narrator will make or break a concept so find a great writer and develop something you are really excited about from the off.

There are lots of excellent books upon this subject and a wealth of talented writers out there; some are lucky enough to work in audio, others are working on coffee shops or advertising or TV. Get yourself one and hash out the story. You're going to have to really trust your production team on this one, as crafting a great story in sound is a skill that takes some honing.

Pros - If you are a brand that's known for doing big, brave, original and adventurous things, and you have a strong social or ethical message to explore, this could work for you. By providing a compelling, immersive, well-told and thought-provoking story, you can not only lead a conversation in your subject area, but bathe in the collective respect of audiences beyond your usual corporate sphere. Do this well and you'll look super cool.

Cons - This isn't the cheapest way to make an audio product. You could be looking at tens of thousands of pounds for a drama but costs will vary depending on the experience of the producers, the duration of the series and the platforms you plan to distribute this across. There are writers, producers, actors, studio facilities, sound designers and highly specialised talent to pay. It's an energy-intensive progress for the team involved and to get a heart and soul response from the audience this medium requires heart and soul writing. It also takes time to write a great script and sound design the finished product.

Do it well by - Remembering that it's okay to be adventurous with drama! Don't let your preconceptions intimidate you. This is a really exciting place to tell stories and there are many firsts to be had at this point in audio history.

Create a really compelling story and characters. Bear in mind that nobody can see your actors or your world as brightly as your mind's eye. Don't swamp your scenes with people that pop up once and disappear, be mindful of your casting so the characters don't get jumbled. This is somewhere bringing in specialist writers, experienced story producers and sound designers will really pay off.

In fiction and scripted narrative, your listeners are choosing to immerse themselves in a whole new world. If they fall in love with that world, they will remember the brand that produces it. This is not the place to shove commercial references into your story. Let the writers write and don't smother them with brand stuff or it will break the magic.

41

If you're choosing to invest in drama then good for you! There are a handful of companies who specialise in this in the UK, but you should listen to a selection of their output before you choose. If you're keen to mix it up and bring in writers who think differently, you might just create a mould-breaking collaboration. In addition to this, making sure you promote the heck out of this gives you the best chance of seeing some sort of traction. Whether you want to put up billboards on the South Circular, plaster the side of a bus, or hire top drawer talent to bring in the fans, if you're investing in making a great series, you should once again be thinking about matching that investment in how you promote it.

Don't forget to ask your actors to advocate for you too, especially if they have big social media followings who might love the show!

A note that applies to any audio production, but may be particularly poignant in the case of dramatised real stories: if you are publishing journalism based on real people's lives, you will need to make sure you don't take unnecessary licence, have permissions where relevant and avoid anything that might appear libellous, slanderous or sensitive. Your producers should be mindful of media law, but involving a specialist from the start is wise.

Whilst we're on this note, a point universal to interviewing guests for media distribution is in having their consent for doing so. Make sure you have the forms signed and that all your participants have given their permission for the manner in which you plan on using their contribution.

If you get into more complex journalism, it's vital to be aware of the laws around consent for recording and privacy rights and it will be worth consulting a trained journalist or legal advisor on best practise.

Montage and Archive

Ever keen to break the mould and push the boundaries, creatives have started having fun with sound in a montage style. Take "The Skewer", for example, which layers news clips and comic writing from a number of sources to create a message or story that's both satirical and ingenious, or the award-winning "Have you Heard George's Podcast", which is basically just art; incorporating storytelling, spoken word, drama, poetry and music as it sees fit.

Alternatively, you might wish to plunge into audio archives to examine old news reports, programmes, interviews or tapes from days of old, leaning on this content to reflect upon the same issues in the current day.

Pros - You can do something truly original by thinking again about how you're using sound, spoken word, music and clips. And as any good story unfolds with more 'show' than 'tell', you can illustrate your points and narrative elegantly with examples and keep the ear of your listener stimulated at the same time. Although podcast listeners tend to dedicate a great deal of commitment in their choices, one long chunk of talk is quite a different experience to something fast-paced and varied. The latter is perhaps more akin to our many-screened lives: attention is everything, so keeping things exciting and diverting matters.

Cons - Licensing could be an issue when using clips from external sources. Some may shrug off the hassle of asking permission or buying rights by declaring their content is published under 'fair dealing'. There is a lot of misunderstanding over what this constitutes. Remember, if you expect your podcast to exist in perpetuity, or if you have a hard time declaring it's satire, you might want to explore the terms of media law before making plans for a whole show where the rights to your content are owned by someone else!

Do it well by - Getting a great sound designer on the case. Balancing and mixing sound from many different sources is a complex job that requires a good pair of ears and a good deal of experience to get right. Also, set aside budget and time to make sure you have the rights secured for any external audio. And whilst you're at it, why not just brush up on your media law.

Immersive Soundscape

Given we've just said how much attentional investment your listener makes when choosing to listen to your podcast episode instead of the millions of other options publicly available, you might be inclined to make it a deeper experience and show off a bit too.

By using sound alone to take them on a journey, you can capture the audience's imagination and transport them to another place. Sound, like any sense, can tap into that special bit of your heart that holds memory and emotion and nostalgia. It can make your hair stand on end and your eyes well up. One sound - be it a birdsong, a piece of music, a door unlocking, or special person's footsteps, can conjure a whole world of reference that is personal and visceral and moving. Furthermore, perhaps because we tend to take our ears for granted more than we do our crashing visual realm, being moved by sound - music, story, a change in voice - can be so delightfully expansive to our awareness of our own senses and capacity.

When we talk about an immersive soundscape, we might mean an atmospheric track of location recordings. But we might also build into this some narrative, be it temporal or physical. You might take someone on a journey - perhaps a walk through a woodland, sparsely narrated. You might hear it as a dramatised depiction of one character's internal experience - the elevator ride, their heavy breathing, the tense office meeting, their frenzied run down the staircase and out into the cool, city air. You can tell a story with sound without stepping outside of the scene, or you could layer in explanation, narration, poetry, even.

Pros - Take someone on a journey without them ever leaving their chair.

Cons - Wind, mostly. But throw in car alarms, tantrumming toddlers and adverse weather for good measure. Making listeners bored is also a risk.

Do it well by - Recording location sound is a specific skill that requires both experience and the right microphones for the conditions. Don't be tempted to cut corners and do it on your iPhone! You might also want to experiment with binaural sound. Sometimes referred to as a "3D" sound, it basically just combines two microphone signals in a spatial arrangement to give the sense of really being 'in' a location - the same room or environment, when listening on headphones. You can get special devices for recording this. With something designed for headphone listening, you naturally won't get the same effect when listening through speakers. In fact if you do listen to binaural on speakers, it probably won't work, so you'll need to make a thing of wearing headphones when marketing your show. Binaural recordings can also be less than easy to listen to when you're doing other things.

The experience can be immersive to the point that the outside world is disruptive, and might make the programme hard to hear.

Narrative Journalism

This crosses over a little with the scripted narrative approach outlined above. This term has been used to describe a manner of reporting real stories through a less-than direct format. It's not so much telling as showing. That is, developing a plot and characters, experimenting with the structure, perspective and manner in which the truth unfolds. It doesn't matter that these are true stories, rather than fiction: the information, narration or manner of storytelling is organised in such a way that it creates intrigue, mystery, poses questions and directs the listener down a certain path and takes them on a journey, perhaps even posing questions that have no clear answer. Just like any good story does. As with any narrative, you can make editorial choices in your structure; what you reveal, what you conceal and what questions you pose and when. Drawing out the complex character of a guest via interview is a great skill. Individuals might all at once be compelling, relatable, flawed or intriguing: which version of them will you present? Are you telling the story responsibly? And can you trust your sources? I know of one major production in recent times which built an incredible narrative series around a source which was later discovered to be bogus. A major embarrassment followed.

Telling human experiences through sound and enjoying the freedom of the format can result in some of the most unique and absorbing programmes. You'll likely need a talented writer or team of writers, a great deal of creative flair and patience, some excellent producers and sound designers. Above all, you'll want a great story as the raw material!

Pros -The most amazing, compelling, surprising, delightful, shocking, gripping, immersive and imaginative use of audio for storytelling is at your fingertips. It's this genre that has created some of the most talked-about and listened-to series in podcasting.

Cons - You can spend a lot of time and money sounding like a rip-off of This American Life.

Do it well by - Personally I find it really awkward to hear British presenters aping Ira Glass. You're not making 'This American Life' so don't be a copycat. Create your own voice and manner of presentation and collaborate with a team to find the most creative and compelling way of unfolding your truth. No two stories are the same, and one story might be told in a multitude of ways. First identify the themes at the heart of the issue, then select the stories and perspectives through which you wish to explore them. You can get help structuring narratives from professional writers and see what devices you could borrow from film, TV and radio. By listening to the many podcasts of this genre you might find inspiration for that crucial question of how to tell a story. You might not be able to do this until you have all the interviews you need, or perhaps one key interview will inform the direction of how your story goes. As with many a piece of journalism, you can start out with one idea of what you want to make, but being open to where the story leads is essential. What sort of stories do you want to be associated with and why are you telling them? Why is this important to your organisation or business? Having a clear sense of this will help you find a path into the forest, and maybe out again!

Once again, ensure all journalism is compliant with respect to the law and personal rights of those featured.

Live Webcast or Event Recording

The numbers of attendees at live events can be limited for all sorts of reasons, especially in an era of global pandemics. But when people are speaking to a live audience, things can happen unexpectedly, off the cuff and uniquely. Being able to bottle that atmosphere and share the highlights with those who didn't make it along in person can maximise the impact your event has.

A public event requires a certain amount of commitment even if it's online. Your attendee typically has to carve out the allotted time in their diary and maybe even travel. They might turn it into a social occasion with friends or colleagues, arriving early and sniffing around in the atrium for a complimentary plastic cup of wine beforehand (maybe that's just me though). Even if they're just making space to sit down at home and listen, the expectation is that your talk is a bit of an event.

Podcasts bring with them their own expectations. For starters, these listeners aren't sitting down at an allotted time to watch or listen to the action. If they didn't have time or inclination to make it along to your original event, then make it easier for them to enjoy your content by repackaging it into a streamlined format. Edit out the bluster and you'll be amazed and how easily a 90 minute talk can become 30.

Pros - More bang for your live event buck: you can increase the reach by packaging the content you've generated into a more widely accessible format.

Cons - That heavy smoker's cough in the front row, poor mic handling by contributors, or clothes noise on mic and the dreaded paper rustle.

Do it well by - Add narration to your podcast to give the talk structure and don't just bash the whole thing out unedited. A podcast gives you the chance to cherry-pick the highlights and most pertinent points from your lecture or discussion, and gives better value to your audience by saving them time and getting to the point faster. Also remember that the long and worshipful introductions given to contributors at events can be done away with in a podcast space. Just a sentence on each contributor and their credentials is enough. You can always put the rest in the show notes. You might even want to add some closing comments, a summing up or conclusion at the end of the podcast.

As for recording, the ideal scenario is one where you have a clean signal for each speaker, which your producer-editor can pull together in the final mix, dropping out unwanted sounds and adjusting the levels or sound for each person as required.

Whether you've decked-out a lecture hall or are broadcasting your event as a live webinar, recording your speakers and audience questions is easy. But then, it's also easy to get it wrong, with so many variables. Whether your contributors are self-recording at home, or have a lapel mic tucked into their jacket, it is sensible to give them a little run-through on mic etiquette before you start. You might want to frame it as an opportunity for them to ask any questions.

Your briefing might include asking them to minimise background noise, avoid too much cross-talking and watch out for noises they can create such as paper rustles or... a bizarre one I often come across: rubbing their knees or scratching their forearms whilst thinking (!). The goal is not to make people self-conscious and inhibited, just to preempt any unwelcome sounds on the recording, so tact and personal judgement is everything when delivering this briefing!

Guidelines for contributors recording themselves from home:

- Use your computer for the interaction and video conferencing software.
- Plug your headphones into the computer so that you can hear the output from other contributors, but your microphone can't!
- Use the smallest room in the house, with the least background noise, and ideally some soft furnishings.
- Record yourself using a smartphone voice memos app, if you do not have a mic
- Ensure the microphone is not too close or too far away from your mouth. 4-6 inches is a rough guide depending on how loudly you speak.
- Do not point your mobile phone microphone directly at your mouth or you might get clipping on some P's or other strong sounds. Instead place it just above or below the line of your breath.
- Try not to move around too much unless your mic goes with you
- Get some 'room tone' that producers can use to remove unwanted noise afterwards if necessary.
- Don't record yourself too loud - check the signal is not distorting on a test recording beforehand. If it's just that you can't hear clearly through your headphones, turn up your headphones, not your microphone!

Guidelines for contributors in a live event scenario:

- Ask contributors to take care not to bash their microphone when the move or gesticulate.
- If they are wearing a lapel mic, position the microphone away from clothes which may move. Equip them with a fluffie to protect it if required.
- If they are holding their mic, this isn't ideal - ask them to be mindful of how close or far away they are holding the mic and coach them on the correct distance to hold it.

- As above, be sure to speak into the microphone! If you are looking around the room or facing another contributor and have a handheld microphone, follow your mouth with your microphone.

Ultimately your guests are there to talk, not to worry about tech, so keeping things as simple as possible with regards live event tech is best. Many live venues have an option to book an engineer to manage this on your behalf using their in-built PA. If your contributors are recording themselves at home, taking a little time to pre-brief them and do a test ahead of the event is worthwhile and will avoid flustering on the night.

Finally, just in case someone forgets to press the big red record button, it's always worth recording a backup. This might be the web feed of your video conference or just a backup mic positioned between the speakers in the room.

Choose your own adventure

Did you ever read those books as a kid where the choices you made on one page took you to a different one on the next? This is the audio alternative! It's fun, engaging, interactive, gimmicky and definitely ambitious, as producers will have to work twice as hard to deliver options for every scenario. But let's face it, that's what producers are doing day-in-day out anyway.

I wanted to include this fairly abstract example because it just goes to show that with regards format and narrative, your imagination is the limiting factor. Podcasting is just a broad term for the manner in which audio programmes and experiences are delivered to an audience. Many of us are used to thinking of audio programmes in terms of radio formats. Personally, with a background originally in radio, this is what I find most enticing and also challenging about the medium: it isn't radio.

From an engineering perspective, this can also be a great delight. The most beloved radio and audio engineers I know are born problem-solvers: thinking outside the box and using the materials available to make something happen and ultimately condense chaos into quality and clarity.

Even radio finds bizarre but effective solutions to making things happen on a budget. One classic example is of course, how to protect your mic from water last minute and on a budget. Until you've seen a handheld mic dressed in the finest Durex can offer, you haven't lived.

Another solution I found to protecting people and kit from contamination following the pandemic was to simply give my microphones their own face masks and change them after every use. Affordable and relatively quick to build into your kit hygiene routine between recordings!

From an engineering and distribution perspective to a creative concept, by letting go of preconceptions of how your programme should be made, you can really push the boundaries of entertainment for your audiences and maybe even make a hit. Okay, business budgets are always going to come into it, but a can-do attitude in your team and the right know-how might just help you make the next big thing.

PLANNING TO DELIVER

Before you start producing anything, it's important to have a plan for how and when you're going to get it to your audience. We'll come on to marketing in the next chapter but here we'll address a few practicalities so you can plan to succeed in making a great show.

You're in a relationship with your audience.

Yeah, that's right. You and your audience are about to embark on a journey that involves good times, faith, trust, loyalty, energy, personal responsibility and most of all fantastic communication.

However, if you don't make the effort to take your audience on a journey, by giving them what they need and managing their expectations, they'll probably just leave you for another shiny new podcast. So keeping a close eye on how they're feeling, what they're telling you and what they're responding to is essential. What's more, you'll need to consider adapting to reflect their changing needs and interests over time.

With any luck, all this energy and care will in return inspire loyalty and passion. Which is the whole point of using podcasts to market your brand, product or business.

So here are my top ten tips for designing your show:

1. FORMAT

Well done, you've got this creative concept nailed, hopefully using the preceding ideas as a jumping off point, or maybe even making up your own. Excited? If not, start again.

2. RELEASE SCHEDULE

Regularity matters. Whether it's once a week, once a month or once a quarter, setting the expectation for when your listeners and subscribers can expect an episode means that they can eventually build a routine listening to your content. If Wednesday is the day they wake up, put the kettle on and see your podcast release in their notifications, Wednesday is the day they associate with getting your show.

Of course, not everyone listens like clockwork. Some people aren't big on a daily or weekly routine, but may enjoy listening to your show in certain place, for example in the gym, or when your partner takes the kids swimming every other Saturday, or catching up on a long car or train journey once a month. Don't disappoint them if they're expecting a bunch of episodes to catch up on and you've not put one out for four weeks. It's hard to build a routine but easy to break it, so don't give your listeners a chance to forget you and always deliver when you say.

3. LONGEVITY OF FORMAT AND ADAPTING TO LEARNINGS

Have you thought about how long you're going to continue releasing your show for?

If you haven't planned a series of specific episodes, or there isn't a pre-planned story-arc to your series narrative, you may plan to carry on releasing ad infinitum. Good for you, but beware the pitfalls. Without planned hinge points in your podcast development you might risk presenters drifting, staff losing momentum, guests flaking or audiences growing bored. Remember, if you're investing in this content as a business you are looking for results. And whilst it might take a while for your listenership to grow and for word to spread, having goals along the way matters. Keeping a close and analytical eye on which episodes get the most listens, social media interactions, news coverage or follow-up interactions (like visiting a webpage or buying a product for example) can give clues as to what is working for your audience.

Reviews can also be a good source of information, although take them to heart at your peril: one swallow does not make a summer and one bad, anonymous review doesn't mean you're doomed. Sometimes it's massively hard to know which analytics to take to heart and which to forget, but they are useful in building up a pattern of understanding as your audience grows and matures. And that's an important point to make. There's a difference between your core audience and those passers-by who might be sampling the latest episode. Keep in mind the focus group of your content and what you want them to believe, feel or do and give each episode a clear purpose in your marketing. Fewer, satisfied interactions are far more useful to your business than 1000 x 2 second interactions because they thought your episode was going to be about something else entirely.

Don't forget to plan for holidays and rest-periods too! If your presenter and team burn out, your audience might fade away too. A well-signalled and planned series break will mean everyone gets to keep it fresh and the passion alive. It also gives you a chance to review what's working and what's not.

A side-note on reviews here. There are lots of services that offer to increase your podcast listener numbers or reviews through some fairy magic. If this is tempting, then I suggest you thoroughly interrogate HOW they plan on doing that for you. Sincere interaction is your goal.

4. WHO AND WHY?

We touched on this earlier (Chapter 1) and it's so important to get this right. Who are you making this show for and why are you making it for them?

There is room for surprises and insights along the way - you are building a brand new concept after all - but anyone who makes content without thinking who they are making it for sets themselves up for failure. In a developing medium, podcast audiences are developing and expanding all the time, but what about your customers? Where do they overlap with podcast listeners? Are you looking to convert non-users into podcast listeners? Or are you looking to speak to existing podcast audiences? It goes without saying that the former will require a lot more work and may have a lower conversion rate.

Thinking about your intended audience's needs will not only influence the kind of content you create for them, it will impact the tone in which you speak to them, the presenter you chose to front your show, how often you release it and when you think they might be most likely to listen. This in turn will impact your whole marketing campaign.

Some businesses might be unsure about this and may want to cast a broad net. Depending on your subject matter a generalist approach can work well, but if a large number of people feel this vanilla approach is "okay" or "it's alright if I'm in the mood", without feeling passionately like it's made just for them, the high water mark that tips them over into subscribers and passionate advocates will remain elusive. Word of mouth and personal recommendation is the most powerful way to help your podcast audience grow, so it's always worth homing in on and marketing to the people you think will love your stuff and be your champions. If your hunch doesn't pay off, you can always re-pivot your approach to explore different demographics and treatments.

That leads us nicely on to the next point.

5. PLAN B

I love Plan B. Plan B happens when you've gone with your first hunch, learned something new and refined your approach. Plan B is targeted and Plan B is wise. If you aren't starting your journey into podcasting with an existing podcast audience, Plan B is when the real magic starts to happen.

It starts like this. With Plan A, you THINK you've got a hit on your hands, but what if this doesn't turn out to be the case? Well, first up it's important to give yourself a reasonable timeline in which to see results. Some shows can catch fire in a week but many others are a slow burn. It's as much to do with marketing as it is the nature of how current and relevant your programme happens to be. If you're working to a niche, specialised audience with specific topics, don't expect the latest Instagram star to be sending her 80k followers to you any time soon (unless she's specialised in the same topic). Instead, consider the value you'd like to deliver to that audience and what this smaller, more self-selecting sample might mean for your business goals. Once you've managed your own expectations and done a little experimentation to gather analytics, it's worth reviewing what you've learned from this.

If you're thinking long-term, or planning future podcast programmes, your first series might be just this: an experiment in not only how this speaks to your audiences but also how it fits with your organisational structure. You will not only learn a lot about your customers through such an experiment but also about how you manage comms across your own business and via the other digital touchpoints in your customer ecosystem.

I guarantee that even if you make the most incredibly far-reaching, award-winning, newsworthy and innovative programme, after series 1 there will be things you want to tweak and improve upon going forwards.

If it's not been quite the success you'd hoped for then all the more so. But it's worth going back to those questions in chapter one and establishing just what success or failure might look like for leg one of your podcast journey and how you're going to measure it.

And like any good experiment, you need to start with a thesis, decide upon your variables, gather data and evaluate this before you conclude what worked for your business and what didn't.

Plan B is an opportunity to pivot to a better product.

6. WHERE WOULD YOU LIKE TO RECORD?

Here's a question that became even more poignant in 2020 when the Coronavirus pandemic saw podcasters scrambling to refine their remote recording setups whilst confined to their homes.

But this has always been one of those questions that can cause a bit of head-scratching, especially if it's one of the last things you do when planning out your programme. Depending on the kind of contributors you are hoping to feature, being round the corner in a production studio, or even in their office can make a big difference to their calendars.

PA FOR THE DAY

As the business end of the production, you will often want to harness your contacts and the relationships you have in your sector to feature in the podcast.

One of the most hectic things about building a podcast programme is the juggle of co-ordinating guest and host calendars. If you start with a host that can spare only one day a month to record a batch of episodes, then you'll already have your work cut out to coordinate guests and locations and hope that nobody's schedule runs over. It can be - to put it mildly - a massive logistical challenge, especially when your energies are also required in researching and refining the programme's content and briefing your presenter. If this is your situation, I'd suggest your options are: 1) Enlist help from a team member with the bookings 2) Hire a producer to make the programme so you can focus on getting the right people in the room 3) Hire a producer to get it all done 4) Work ALL the hours to get it done yourself. Much will depend upon the flexibility of your contributors too.

THE RIGHT PLACE AND TIME

If calendars aren't an obstacle, that frees you up to focus on creating the right environment. You may want to record in your office. You may want to record in a high-end studio with a viewing gallery. You may want to record up a mountain or walking along the beach. You might want to walk around a museum or tour the factory or shop floor. When picking a recording location you should consider three things:

1. What is the value or recording here? Is this going to add a little something to your show? Will your guests be able to respond to the objects in their environment? Will you be able to record background SFX to help the listener feel like they are there and to give a sense of place? How important is that sense of place to what you are trying to convey? Perhaps you are recording on location simply because it's easier for everyone involved to get there. In which case, your second point is raised:

2. How will this location impact the value of the interaction? If you are doing an interview, how might your presenter and guests respond to their environment? How might they respond differently in that environment? This is really important to consider, as a chilly, distracted presenter or a guest who feels they're under-dressed for a interview might not create the most focussed and engaging conversation. They might miss things or come across stilted or stressed. Which doesn't add up to a great listen.

3. What do I need to do to get a good-quality sound in this location? This might include a pre-recording visit to identify potential problems, for example background noise, weather or wind conditions. All of which can be worked around and mitigated with the right planning and the right kit.

REMOTE RECORDING

Once utilised mostly by people separated by oceans or impossible calendars, remote recording was a god-send for the booming podcast industry in 2020. From corporate leaders to doctors to celebrities, for a time, the world was confined to its homes but the technology used to support this remote working also enabled a boom in activities previously performed outside the home. As a result there was a surge in content creation, as we all sought to connect with the worried world at large. We found ourselves invited into Arnie's kitchen, meeting the cats of Hollywood celebs, or just seeing what art that platinum pop star has on the wall. What's more, with many public activities suspended, suddenly there was a big increase in the availability of talented performers to make ad-hoc appearances on podcasts, adding to the trend that had already begun in this space, of established talent using the medium to curate and create personal, intimate and 'authentic' content.

And whilst 'personal' and 'authentic' may be overused expressions, their relevance still stands. However shiny and well-curated, a willingness in presenters, hosts and podcast guests to be candid is not only fashionable, it seems to have become a requirement of the medium. People 'get' that these programmes are listened to by individuals, mostly privately, on headphones in their personal time. Podcasts have become a safe space to talk about mental health and other previously taboo subjects. Indeed the diversity of topics that now exist, with everyone seeking their own niche, means that you're hard pressed not to find a podcast about any topic under the sun.

Which is why location matters, not only in creating a comfortable space for conversations to take place, but also in the manner in which they are listened to.

There isn't anything good about a global pandemic, but what COVID-19 has inspired is the brilliance of human ingenuity in finding new ways to support communication amongst previously indifferent or older user groups.

Nowadays it doesn't have to be the end of the world if your guests can't be in the same room. Whilst the traditional face-to-face meeting feels most intimate, we've all been forced by social distancing to explore alternative ways to present ideas or have thoughtful conversations. We have learned how to have quality conversations even when we are miles apart.

What's more, necessity has forced us to create better sound quality for these interactions too. It used to be that recording a phone call in phone quality was the accepted but last-ditch option if you couldn't get that guest on a microphone. Well, it's still last-ditch, but today you have a few choices before that. Video conferencing and Amazon door to door delivery in addition to the fantastic little microphones sitting in every smartphone users pocket means that as long as you can walk your guests through self-recording, you can walk your way to a decent-sounding show.

In short, location is about creating the right atmosphere and mood for the conversation to take place. That means that you want your guests to be comfortable, confident and not distracted by the technology. If that means the best way to do your interview is with everyone on a video call from their favourite sofa, then so be it.

7. HOW WILL THIS PODCAST BE USEFUL?

We talked in part one about defining the change you want your podcast to generate. To recap, you might think you're looking for increased loyalty in a certain audience towards your brand, a certain kind of emotion, or even action towards visiting a website, using an offer code or purchasing a product or service. But in order for a podcast to be useful to you in this sense, it first needs to be useful to your user.

A firm understanding of the needs and lifestyle of your target customer is therefore essential in creating something that will improve and change their world in its own right. This model of giving a little before you get, means that goodwill towards your brand is the channel through which you'll see results. Whether you want to change perceptions or create action based on existing ones, emotion is key, and that means thinking about how you can solve your audience problems.

Don't just think about traditional podcast formats here. With the increasing integration and use of smart speakers and voice technology in our homes, cars and pockets, creating short-form content to answer questions, or long-form content to explain subjects can be a simple and functional way of embedding yourself into routines, whether its a kind of news bulletin or flash update or an explainer series to common questions say, if you were a DIY homestore, to common DIY questions.

"Alexa, how do I change a lightbulb?"

You get what I mean?! You can make this content available on as many platforms as you like, so why limit yourself to one?

A note on numbers here though - even if you make the perfect programme for your target audience, don't expect them all to listen. Not everyone in the population uses podcasts or even knows how to use them. I still get questions about filming and crew[*] when fixing up some location recordings or approaching contributors. Not everyone knows what the deal is with podcasting. Ultimately, only a percentage of your target audience will be willing to listen to or use podcasts, and you need to make sure they know it exists too.

[*]That's not to say 'filming' your podcast is a bad idea. Video can actually generate some useful content for marketing the show on visual comms channels, but does add a whole other layer of planning to your recording scenario.

Back to the 'how will this podcast be useful' question. Even if you have the best marketing in the world, and a perfectly designed campaign to get people listening, they'll only come back if it's good. That means the topics, the treatment, the talent and total package needs to make them feel good. Whether that 'good' means more informed, intelligent, entertained, amused, intrigued, excited, turned-on... whatever, is up to you. Your job is to make something that gives that audience what they need and makes it easy for them to access, not only in how you distribute your podcast but how you package it and even how you market it to be listened to, for example, whilst on a walk, commute or cooking.

The important thing is not to be limited by the subject matter of what your brand or company provides, but to give the audience something useful that starts to solve their problem. Everyone is busy these days. And even if they're not, their time is still valuable and you should respect it, especially if you're asking them for more and more of it!

An example here:

Bank A and Bank B both sell homeowner loans and want to target upwardly-mobile young families who want to improve not move.

Bank A creates a round-table programme where their various directors and staff discuss the financial options available for people who want to improve their homes, borrow for big projects or plan for their retirement. Generally this programme leaves the listener feeling better informed and aware of their financial options for specific circumstances.

Bank B creates a series featuring stories and interviews with people who have made their dream homes on a budget. It's hosted by a favourite comedian or presenter of their target demographic and is full of great ideas, tips, horror stories and funny moments where people laugh in the face of tough times and come through. Generally it leaves the listener feeling like family and home is the most important thing and together you can make amazing things happen.

If you're an upwardly-mobile young parent who is juggling work, kids and DIY projects all at once, what sounds like a more enjoyable listen for your precious personal time? It's Bank B's. Although Bank A does sound useful, the content it likely to be less exciting to listen to and less of an easy habit to keep, even for the most dedicated self-educator. After a long day, they might just fall off the wagon and listen to Joe Rogan whilst sanding that floor instead. AND, even if Bank B doesn't give you the nitty gritty on interest rates and eligibility criteria for their loans, a quick direction to Bank B's website and maybe even an offer code can point them in the right direction. The difference between Bank A and Bank B doing that at the end of the show is that Bank B has already done its sales work by creating the right emotional connection with its listeners. Even if Bank B's numbers aren't quite as good, they've shown they understand what the customer is all about: family and home is the most important thing and together you can make amazing things happen.

In this context, a useful podcast is both functional and emotional to its audience. However, as you may have noticed in those examples, getting the content right is only half of the job. Picking the talent that has influence in your audience demographic can be a really smart move too. Which leads us to the next question.

8. HOW WILL THIS BE USEFUL TO AS MANY PEOPLE AS POSSIBLE?

A general lifestyle brand example now:

Brand A and Brand B provide the same products and have the same target audience. Their target audience are moderate to heavy social media users, watch TV and are generally engaged with mainstream culture. This is a generic example, but presumes that the target audience has an interest in the celeb personalities picked to host.

Brand A hires a celeb presenter with a massive online following to interview interesting and well-known TV & film personalities about their home lives. The conversations aren't particularly heavily edited, but they're compelling listening by virtue of who the people involved are, and what the guests have to say.

Brand B hires a celeb presenter who doesn't do social media to interview ordinary people about their extraordinary home lives and stories, with expert advice and analysis on their situations. They're all recorded at home for that particularly intimate feel.

Although Brand A's concept is simpler to execute and perhaps less thoughtful than Brand B's, it's likely to reach more people because:

1) The celeb presenter actively uses social media and, presuming you have agreed they will promote their podcast, will help immediately to spread the word to people who are already interested in what they do.

2) The guests involved are immediately more interesting to the target audience than someone they have no prior reference for and therefore have to work harder to care about in the first place. It's not to say that the celeb story is more interesting or worthwhile than the unknown person, it's just more immediate because of their existing notoriety.

Even if the content produced by Brand B is far superior and more useful, Brand A has invested more promotional budget in a talent that will champion their product to their own broad audience on social media, thus making the butterfly effect of its advocates larger. Reach, reach, reach! Plus, their celeb guests might even promote it to their networks too, which just happen to include plenty more people from your target audience. In this example Brand B hopes that their audience will do the advocating to their networks, or indeed that their guest's story will catch some press coverage, but Brand A has their celeb's network to do this for them and knows their talent is already a regular headline-filler.

This is just an example of why the simple celeb-led format can be successful: intimacy, sincerity, emotion and insight are a lynchpin of these formats, especially when dedicated followers and fans are involved. That's not to say that you need a well-known and active presenter with a strong social following to present your podcast though. You can still make a great product and with a great presenter, even if they don't have a big reach online. If that's the case you may need to invest a little more promotional money and energy in other ways. Ultimately the show still has to be interesting and useful for people to identify with it and want to share it.

9. SOUND AND FURNITURE

The language and style of your presenter, as well as the music and sounds used all impact the way someone feels when they listen to your show, so considering brand sound before you start is worthwhile. Building sound into your show planning will help add structure and build expectation as the series goes on. It also balances changes of energy throughout your episode, and can help with any awkward transitions!

You may want to use music to move from different features or create a feeling. Think about how your theme will create the right energy for the programme too. At the start of the show you'll always need to re-set the concept and set the context for new listeners who might have just stopped by, in addition to doing a menu of what will be covered in the episode and why it matters.

In radio, imaging and sound design is there to give an instant sense of identity to the station, unique to them, even if they're playing the same songs as the other channel. In podcasting, you listener is more likely to have consciously selected a programme, rather than just switching on and picking up with the station they left off with, so your sound is more to create a certain mood and familiarity with your audience. Your organisation may even have a brand sound already, for different areas of your advertising and marketing. Consider whether you might be able to adapt this theme to a new context, or whether you'd like to keep things distinct.

There are now many quality music libraries providing high-end, polished sounds, royalty-free, for a subscription fee. Whether it's an emerging band, classical composer or spare bedroom-based beats maker, musicians are making and licensing music using the power of the web. Some provide the stems of tracks too, so that you can keep the theme but adapt different layers of instruments for a different feeling.

What's more, libraries have recognised that podcasters might not want to pay the same fee for their podcast usage as large international broadcasters and have introduced more flexible pricing structures.

The fashions for these libraries seem to ebb and flow, so if you're using a popular one, always consider your theme carefully and don't just pick the first one on the list! It's always a bit weird to hear a piece of music you've used pop up in a different context on the telly.

There are also libraries that allow you to purchase an annual track licence for a one-off fee.

Others might be covered by the MCPS rate card which can be found here:

https://www.prsformusic.com/-/media/files/prs-for-music/licensing/production-music/production-music-rate-card-01-2020.pdf

You can browse their libraries here:

https://www.prsformusic.com/licences/using-production-music

With any licensed piece of music there may be further conditions associated with its use i.e. crediting the artist or referencing them in the podcast description or otherwise, so be sure to read the fine print to make sure you're covered:

Here are just a few links to get you started, correct as at January 2021.

AudioNetwork
https://www.audionetwork.com

Artlist
https://artlist.io

Premiumbeat by Shutterstock
https://www.premiumbeat.com/

Free Music Archive
https://freemusicarchive.org/

Tribe of Noise Pro
https://prosearch.tribeofnoise.com

Marmoset
https://www.marmosetmusic.com

Audiosocket
https://audiosocket.com

Epidemic Sound
https://www.epidemicsound.com

Blue Dot Sessions
https://www.sessions.blue

You might also want to consider commissioning a bespoke piece for your programme, seeking out a composer to turn your brief into a sound nobody else will have. It's helpful to give composers some reference tracks if you're doing this and to tell them what you like about them, whether it's the instruments used, mood, pace, or a certain arrangement.

10. ADVERTISING

By now you might have realised that the process of creating your podcast is a piece of your organisation's wider marketing strategy. The content creation and the needs of your listener are - or should be - unified. We live by the numbers and there's nowhere to hide in podcasting! Money spent funding an audio programme is always either an investment on behalf of the funder or the funder's customers. The value for the business lies in increased loyalty to the business and a fulfilling of part of its remit, whether that business is a broadcaster, a commissioner or a tax-funded public body. As a producer, it's possible to make beautiful, fun things on someone else's dollar, but without either a good reach amongst core customers or good critical acclaim or PR, it's unlikely to be repeated. There must be a solid business case.

I'm not knocking podcasting as a hobby, by the way. Just pointing out the difference between paid-for creation and art for art's sake: the former tends to be about the person listening, the latter about the person making it!

So far we've thought about the audience, their needs and problems and how we're going to solve them in order to make your business look good and win their loyalty.

The next vital component in the marketing process is how to advertise it (see Chapter 6). Advertising can take many forms, but whatever form you choose the goal is always the same: to make your audience aware of your podcast and how it will benefit them.

A valid question at this point would be: If I'm investing in advertising my podcast, why don't I just advertise my core business product instead?

And the answer to that question is that your podcast is now one of your products too. This is a product that creates pure emotion. It may be that the brand of deodorant you make or the projects your charity works on are the best, but if you don't make people feel it is something special that stands out from others, they may never a) try it or b) tell their friends.

That means that like any other product or service you supply your podcast will aim to build an ongoing relationship with the person using it, or else establish itself as relevant to them for as long as they have the need you're trying to meet. It will also act as a vehicle to establish hopefully positive emotions and opinions in the user about your products and services and convert them from casual samplers to loyal repeat customers.

Traditional advertising opportunities also exist for podcasts, but depending on what other channels you have available. Here are a few that could be used as part of your marketing mix to get the word out.

- Cross-promotion on your other products, such as TV, Radio, magazines
- Billboard campaigns.
- Online advertising, including popups that open the audio in your podcast app.
- Email, including links in your regular newsletters to subscribers who like your other products and might enjoy this one.
- Some podcast platforms and companies also sell advertising across other programmes. These campaigns will play your advert to certain categories of audiences on the proviso that if they find one show interesting, they might like yours. This is sold on an impact basis at a cost per thousand rate. That means you pay an agreed amount per every number of listeners the ad is served to. It doesn't take into account how long they listen or whether they take action, so it's important to design a catchy creative. More on this later on.
- Paid-for promotion on other podcasts via host-read ads or reviews.
- Sponsorship of other podcasts.
- Paid social advertising

If there is already a wealth of digital audience insight within your organisation, bear in mind that your podcast audience may still not be a blueprint of the ones you've already identified in other places. You are building a brand new audience in addition to those who are already digitally-engaged with you.

As for social media campaigns, you can create all sorts of awesome assets to spread the word out about your podcast to platforms that already have audiences, and to build conversations around your content. In this way an ongoing programme might build up a sort of symbiosis with social channels, feeding interactions and subject matter back and forth and dealing with them in different ways - the podcast long-form, the social for quick hits. You may find your social impressions are way higher than your podcast listens, but don't be disheartened. It's the difference between someone's full, committed attention for 20 minutes as they lean in and the passing hit of a scroll through social feeds. Both are valuable in their respective ways and can work together as a bigger, integrated marketing campaign that benefits your business.

If you want to find out more, skip to section 6 where we'll also go through your best practise to setting up for a hit.

Now, let's get down to the nitty gritty.

PART 3 - PRODUCERS, SOFTWARE & KIT

- **What a producer does**
- **When to invest and when to hire**
- **Getting started as a do-it-yourself podcaster**
- **Sound and kit basics**

This is where this beautiful thing you have previously imagined in your head is turned into something tangible for others to hear and enjoy. It's the bit after development. We call it production, although all the theory you've done up to this point is as much a part of production as the technical stuff we're about to talk about.

WHAT IS A PRODUCER?

At this point, you may have decided bring in a specialised producer to help bring your concept to life. The title 'producer' can get very confusing and doesn't always give you the best insight into the skillset of the person or company you're hiring to help. As in any other industry, the word producer literally just means someone who makes things. That can involve a whole lot of different skills!

If you've brought in a podcast or audio production company this may mean the business is able to offer a wide range of services.

Below are 40 examples of services a podcast producer or podcast production company might offer, depending on the needs of the project. I've tried to put them in a logical order of when these services might be required during a project lifecycle. In reality, some tasks will run simultaneously or on an ongoing basis.

Some companies or freelancers may help with a few aspects of the process, others may offer a full service depending on how hands on you are and how much resource and expertise you have available – and wish to use - within your business already. Always make sure you discuss exactly what you'd like an external producer to deliver as part of your contract so that you can plan costs and timelines accordingly together. It's key to make sure you integrate a smooth workflow early on so that everyone knows what they're responsible for, and your colleagues are able to plan for any podcast-related activities such as consultations with producers, feedback and social media integration.

40 TASKS WITHIN THE PRODUCTION PROCESS:

1. Responding to your business brief with a creative proposal
2. Consulting on and designing your programme, series and concept.
3. Designing your marketing campaign.
4. Designing and managing timelines for production on an ongoing basis.
5. Advising on how to measure success against your business criteria.
6. Advising on budgets for your programme.
7. Working with your staff to identify how the podcast will be managed and used throughout the business.
8. Consulting with you to understand your target audience and their needs.
9. Researching and planning content.
10. Writing programmes and incorporating feedback
11. Adapting the tone and style of content to the level of the audience
12. Integrating commercial messages in a comfortable, personable way that doesn't feel overtly pressured.
13. Advising on where and how is best to incorporate commercial messaging.
14. Entering awards.
15. Training and briefing presenters.
16. Negotiating with talent agents to find the right presenter for the job.
17. Handling presenter contracts.
18. Getting presenters coffee / lunch / hairdryers and managing personal needs of guests.
19. Booking taxis, hotels or transport.
20. Helping identify talent within your organisation.
21. Sourcing guests and contributors from outside your organisation.
22. Advising on any kit you may wish to purchase.
23. Supplying kit and recording audio in the chosen location, perhaps also even recording video.

24. Directing presenters, guests and contributors throughout recording.
25. Finding and booking studios and recording locations where required.
26. Carrying out health and safety checks for recording, and risk assessment / mitigation controls.
27. Providing insurance for the recording.
28. Ensuring material is compliant for 'air', meets the legal requirements of rigorous journalism and managing personal data in a GDPR compliant manner.
29. Editing and producing your programmes and maybe even video.
30. Briefing and handling negotiations for bespoke music creation.
31. Licensing music for use in your programmes.
32. Licensing or clearing any clips and handling rights to other audio content in your programme.
33. Ensuring licensed material is correctly credited in programme descriptions or online as required.
34. Presenting you with options for hosting your podcast.
35. Handling uploads and distribution via your podcast host.
36. Working with web and social teams to brief or create social assets.
37. Writing search engine optimised episode descriptions and promotional materials.
38. Advising on how best to advertise your podcast.
39. Creating and managing ads.
40. Delivering reports and analysis of listener numbers to track with your KPIs.

Whilst this is by no means an exhaustive list, there are a lot of varied tasks within the production process which may require some outside help! There can be more to the job than meets the eye, so having a trusted producer or company on board to take care of the detail can free you up to it focus on the big picture.

WHEN TO INVEST AND WHEN TO HIRE?

Whereas this book aims to arm you with the knowledge and questions to navigate these points and the crucial strategic questions for a successful podcast, an experienced producer or production company can do the leg work and offer the support and expertise on tasks as and when you want (and need) it.

Your production company might be a font of knowledge on all of these things, and probably a whole lot more. Your producer might have a broad range of individual skills and experiences, but do bear in mind they may also be highly specialised.

If you are hiring an individual, do make sure that you get a clear picture of just what services they have experience in providing so that you don't find yourself taking on more than you bargained for. It's always worth agreeing just what your producer is going to do and how you will work together in a contract before the job starts. This will protect you both.

Otherwise, it's up to you how much time and energy you are prepared to put into making your business's podcast a success. Having someone within the organisation at least to liaise between stakeholders, staff and departments is a must, even if you are hiring in help for the more specialised stuff. Bear in mind that anyone external you bring into your business will need to understand the unique needs and issues and structure of your organisation if they're to effectively market it, so having one of your own to oversee this at the start is essential.

You may be fortunate enough to find that you have a former radio or podcast producer or audio engineer working in your organisation, or perhaps a digital department that is experienced in audio. In the age of the multi-skilled worker it's rare but not impossible that you might have sitting in your organisation the perfect person for the job. Even so, you'll need to invest in their time as well as providing them with the best tools for the job.

HIRING A PRODUCER

Hiring a producer may have you wondering where to begin. There are countless companies and individuals to be found with a little Google search, so it's worth having an idea of the sort of programme you'd like to create to help narrow your search. Asking a top entertainment producer to make your art history programme, or putting a music specialist onto hard politics might work out, but it's probably better to find out about the specialisms of companies first! You could do this by looking up the production companies behind programmes you admire, or even asking your professional network for recommendations on companies or individuals with a similar background.

Many programmes have credits at the end for production companies (although not always). This is common in BBC radio programmes, for example, but not so much with independent or branded content. A bit of detective work on Google might help you figure out a company's involvement. Failing that, picking up the phone and asking the commissioner outright for the name of the production company used and their opinion is the obvious next step!

Even running production company I find it hard to get a clear view of a new freelance producer's skillset from CV or website alone. Asking for some links to shows they've made, and details of the work they did (for example writing, research, editing, development, marketing) will give you the best idea of who and what you're signing up for. Have a chat with them about their creative process by all means, especially if you will be asking them to put a lot of heart, soul and thought into what you're making. Perhaps they will also be open to doing a trial run or consultation to see if they are the right fit for your organisation and the project.

The right person or company can be worth their weight in gold. The ability to adapt viewpoint and tone to a brand might be a priority for you, but you may also be looking for something a little more independent in the way you present your content. Working out this editorial relationship and making it clear who has the final say is important when works of great art are in the making!

There are networks of fantastic podcast producers who are happily sharing tips and jobs with one another here in the UK. Podcasting, even though it's now good business for some of the bigger media houses, remains a generous and vibrant place for freelancers. There are lots of skilled audio people with different interests and backgrounds out there, sharing in a common a passion for making a great programme. You may also be surprised how helpful you find individual producers once you have an open and honest chat about your needs. Rates have also progressed to becoming more standardised in recent years, as the audio market has become a little less volatile and irregular, allowing you to make decisions based on the right person or company, and not a wide disparity in price.

INVESTING IN TECHNOLOGY

Many companies I speak to have taken advice on what kit to buy in such circumstances where they want to keep costs low and use internal staff to do the job of a producer. For simple projects, the software now available makes it now technically quite reasonable for someone of little experience to record and publish a programme. Indeed in certain circumstances many of us now walk around with a fairly decent little microphone in our pocket - in the form of the modern smartphone.

This is where we get to one of those divisive questions: how important is it to sound 'good'.

Whilst a great quality sound, the right recording environment, seamless editing and experience in programming for specific audiences is by no means a pre-requisite to publishing a podcast, and never has been, the programme you publish does very much reflect upon your energy and resources as a business. And since we are ultimately making branding for your business or organisation, let's make sure we give you the best possible chances of sounding good.

A lot goes in to making a quality production and much of that takes place before you hit the record button. There are several things to consider to ensure your physical sound is good which we'll cover in more detail shortly. For the rest of this chapter, let's start with a little overview of what kind of equipment is used for recording, editing and publishing your programme. So what does your average recording setup look like, in terms of kit?

In the most traditional sense, you will need a microphone to pick up sound, cables or some other means to transmit to your recorder, a recorder to receive and save the sound to your chosen format, and a variety of cables to get it to your computer or editing programme.

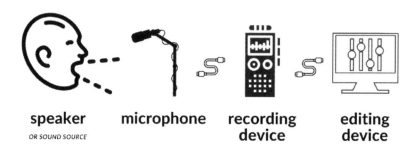

speaker   **microphone**   **recording**   **editing**
OR SOUND SOURCE   **device**   **device**

EXAMPLE OF A TRADITIONAL RECORDING PROCESS

ALL IN ONE TOOLS

Apps and web programmes such as Anchor and Alitu allow you to do all of the above and make a podcast with just your mobile phone or computer. Some even go as far as incorporating other media asset creators such as Headliner, an app that lets you make video content to promote your podcast.

With quality microphones built-in to most modern smartphones these days, you can use these apps to can record, carry out basic editing and even publish. You might require little more than your index finger to make a podcast. If that's for you, then bon voyage! Much like website-builders, and online graphic design template programmes, these take out the technicalities of creation for beginners and allow you to make simple creations on a budget. They certainly don't put programmers or artists out of jobs, and nor do these apps pose a threat to trained audio-producers. Indeed most of the sophisticated audio-editing programmes and technology used today merely ape the bigger, clunkier creations of the past. When the Beatles and Rolling Stones were making 4-track recordings in the 1960s by layering multiple different takes of their songs, they did not know that today we would be able to do this with one device, held in the palm of your hand, nor digitally via a laptop computer. That's with the exception of Mick Jagger, of course, who we all know is capable of time travel.

74

Anyway, to those curious and interested in more complex productions, please read on!

The first part of getting a decent recording is not, in fact, good kit. It's a good space and good practise. Without these even the fanciest bit of kit won't live up to its calling.

THE BASICS OF SOUND

Here's a simplified overview of how sound works.

Sound is vibration, and these vibrations travel as waves.

All sound is, is energy moving molecules in a certain manner, which is then picked up by the little hairs in your ear and converted to electrical signals which are then processed by your brain into the marvellous thing we perceive to be a symphony, a baby laughing, the wind in the trees, or whatever. The form and behaviour of those waves depends upon the composition of the things bouncing off each other on their way to your ears.

Some sounds are direct, meaning they get to your ears and you hear them directly. Reflected sounds arrive later, having bounced off objects and walls. Your microphone, like your ear, will pick these up and this will influence the overall sound.

You know when you walk into a church and shout, it's going to sound and feel very different to shouting the same thing underwater, or under the duvet on your bed. You also know that when your neighbour at number 32 is playing drum and bass through the wall at midnight, it sounds and feels very different to the opera lilting through the open-air park recital.

Thud, thud th-thu-th-thud. Ah, next door are listening to Pendulum again.

To explain this, first know that the human ear picks up a narrow range of sound frequencies. These are the frequencies we work with when we work with sound design and audio production. And what's more as you get older and those hairs fall out or your ears block up or other stuff happens to your ear receivers, you begin to hear a narrower range of frequencies.

In short, the sound that your microphone picks up will be influenced by the number and nature of things it bounces off before the sound reaches the microphone.

There are several steps to consider in getting the right sound for your recording:

- Room / Location
- Microphone
- User

Room

Depending what sound you want to create, you then need to consider the shape, size and composition of the room and the objects in it. The higher the ceilings or bigger the room, the longer the reverberation time.

Every room has a different ambient sound or tone, too. Try recording 'silence' in your hallway, kitchen or bathroom and you'll notice that you still pick up a different texture of fuzziness.

Materials make a difference to the acoustics of a room. Different surfaces absorb and reflect sound differently. Hard objects are generally more reflective. Windows let sound in, too. Corners, mirrors, windows and bare walls can make for unpleasant sound reflections, more echo and more noise. Soft surfaces like rugs, curtains and acoustically-padded walls make for a deader sound and dampen or deflect the reflections. What would you prefer to listen to on a podcast? With all recording locations you look for the best possible conditions. That's why professional recording studios have all that pointy foam up the walls (or egg-boxes for the home-made solutions!).

Home or Office Recording

If you want a clear, clean sound without too much ambient noise for your mic to pick up, the first step is to go for a small room with lots of soft things on the walls and low ceilings. Listen out for outside noise and try to minimise that. Drywalls are generally better at keeping this out that plasterboard.

Please note standard curtains are not a professional alternative to sound-treated walls so don't pay through the nose for them just because they're branded as 'acoustic'! You'd be better off using an old duvet and spending the cash elsewhere.

Sound engineering can be a highly specialised skill, but there is no right or wrong environment for making sound, only the best possible conditions for the sound you're trying to create, so it's worth experimenting with the spaces you have available.

Don't make the mistake of mixing up the term "sound-dampening" with "sound-proofing" either. Sound-proofing means literally that. You can't hear through something sound-proof as this requires preventing sound entering a space in the first place. It's very hard to achieve. It's also unlikely that you will require a sound-proof environment for your recording. Installing and creating such an environment is highly specialised, technical and expensive. It's also probably quite unnecessary for your investment.

Dampening the sound in a home or office environment can be done on the cheap by hanging spare curtains, duvets or rugs, and placing rugs over hard surfaces. You can also buy acoustic foam by the square which may be useful in some spots. In professional studios you might see this on the walls, with lots of pointy shapes at funny angles. These objects absorb reflections, or diffuse them by scattering the sound in different directions. If you decide to defile your spare room in the honourable pursuit of a quiet recording space, these may look ugly, but on the plus side provide a talking point when your cousin Derek comes to stay.

The above criteria are useful to consider in any recording scenario in order to get the clearest vocal sound, but obviously if you want to capture the authentic sound of recording on location then that's a different story.

Sometimes though, the easiest option for the best sound is to simply hire a professional recording studio. Some will even provide you with an engineer so that you can turn your attention to what's being said and not worry about how it sounds!

Microphones

Recording into your mobile phone might be handy in a crisis, but a quality podcast deserves a quality microphone, not to mention something that has a comfortable stand, popshield or windshield option if you need it.

The good news is that these days the best manufacturers have been working hard to create microphones that make recording in almost any location a cinch, even for beginners. But buying a microphone can still feel like a big step, and with lots of terminology surrounding them, it's hard to know what's what.

You personal preference for sound is a big factor in choosing a mic, as different kinds have different sounds. The practicality of what sort of programme you are making also informs your decisions, whether it's one person speaking into a laptop from the kitchen table or a round-table discussion with many voices.

Once again, for amateur podcasters and seasoned producers alike, the goal is to get the best and clearest sound possible for the environment, with the least fuss and the most flexibility. Let's look at the options now:

Connection: How to get the signal into your recording device.

If you record straight into a computer or are solo and generally stay in one place when you're recording, a USB-connected mic could be a straightforward option. This can also work if you have contributors in different locations, all separately recording their own voices for stitching together afterwards, perhaps using a video chat to enable the discussion and record a backup.

For more complex situations, for example, if you have several different people in one location and want to record their voices separately on separate mics, you use microphones with an XLR connection to an interface or mixer which will allow you to adjust their signals independently. In addition to the 'interface' or recording device you might need to buy the XLR cable separately, whereas most USB microphones come with the connecting cable built in.

In addition to these options, you can also get recorders with built-in microphones to make life super easy. Some of these are useful for recording solo, others for putting in the middle of the table to pick up a circle of sound around them. That's why the next consideration is your mic's direction.

<u>Direction</u>

This matters because a mic's direction (polarity) defines how sensitive it is to sound in a three-dimensional space.

Omnidirectional or multidirectional microphones record a circular field around the microphone. They're great for field recording, for example when you want to capture the sound of a location, or when your subject doesn't stay still! They are also good for recording a wide source, for example a large group of people or instruments. This is the kind of mic you could have in the middle of a round-table. It would pick up the voices of the speakers, but also the background noises. In that scenario your speakers will likely all be a little distance from the mic too, so you probably won't get a crisp, clean vocal.

Bidirectional microphones (also known as figure 8) record in two opposing directions. They're useful for recording two guests facing one another as the mic will be most sensitive to these two points and pick up less of the surrounding noise.

Cardioid or unidirectional microphones record on one side - the area in front of the mic - most sensitively. They take in a little bit to the sides, and ignore what's behind them. This is great for recording one speaker who is directly in front of the microphone. It will cut down on the location sound recorded and focus clearly on the voice in front of it. You can also get different levels of sensitivity in cardioid microphones. They're a good options for recording a speaker in rooms that are not sound-treated, like your average home or office, but it does mean your speaker has to be disciplined in not moving away from the mic (and thus out of the sensitivity field) if they get carried away chatting. Another feature of both bidirectional and cardioid mics is that when you get closer the sound becomes extra intimate and bassy, something that's known as the Proximity Effect. Quite nice really, but only when you want it.

In terms of desk mics, the kind you find in a seated studio setup, if you were to look at your mic in a 360-degree space, this diagram gives an idea of the sound field they are sensitive to.

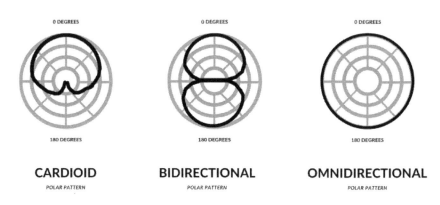

REPRESENTATION OF POLAR PATTERNS IN 360 SPACE

Condenser or Dynamic?

We're nearly there with the technical terms!

Another thing you might see referred to on your mic specification relates to the technical manner in which they capture sound.

Condenser microphones have an electrically-charged diaphragm. When this vibrates acoustically they convert this to an electrical current. As they are electrically-charged, they usually need a power source. This might be via Phantom power (48 volts) delivered from the mixer or recording device down the XLR cable, which is sending the sound signal in the other direction back to the recorder. This means they generate a louder output than dynamic mics. Condenser mics are good for recording vocals because of their power and sensitivity. They might have a specifically large or small diaphragm. The difference here is in how focussed the diaphragm is on certain frequencies. For voice, often large diaphragm condenser microphones can be preferable because they give a wide, loud sound and you aren't as prone to lose lower frequencies if moving around.

Dynamic microphones use electromagnetism to turn sound into a signal. A coil within a magnet picks up the vibration and moves within a magnet to create a voltage. They don't need power input and are good for recording loud inputs. They're can give you a smooth vocal without being overly sensitive. In comparison to condenser mics they're less likely to pick up every sound in the atmosphere. They're also generally a bit tougher if you drop them!

Both dynamic and condenser mics can be great for recording voices and once again, it's all about finding the right mic for your particular recording situation.

Personal Preference

In addition to finding the mic that gives you the best convenience and flexibility for your scenario, you might have opinions on how you want to sound too. As I mentioned earlier every kind of mic has a unique sound. Once you've whittled down your list of appropriate mics to a shortlist, do get onto YouTube and listen to some of the comparison videos that exist. I find this so helpful in consolidating a final decision before buying a microphone. You could of course go old school and go into a specialist store to try out microphones and speak one to one with a professional, but I know it's not always possible these days! I recommend the fantastic staff at West End Production in London who have never failed to help me make a good decision over the years.

What's hot right now?

In trying to make the principles of this book as applicable at any time as possible, I've not given too many time-sensitive recommendations. Technology is changing rapidly with new options hitting the market all the time. However, at the time of writing, here are a few mics that are certainly very useful in podcasting and which may be a great start for your research:

Blue Microphones: Yeti - a USB condenser microphone available in a range of colours. You can select whichever recording mode suits, too, from omnidirectional to bidirectional, cardioid and stereo mode.

Rode USB microphones: Both of these cardioid, USB connected condenser mics are very straightforward to use.

NT-USB - condenser microphone with a sensitive, neutral sound.
Podcaster- Designed specifically for spoken voiceovers designed to mimic a classic radio sound. The frequency response is narrower and it's less sensitive than the NT-USB so you need to sit a little closer. It has a built-in pop shield.

Rode Procaster - a dynamic cardioid mic with built-in pop shield. This connects via XLR so is a little less entry-level. Otherwise the main difference from the Podcaster is a more natural sound.

Audiotechnica's AT2020USB+ is a cardioid condenser USB microphone designed to allow you to plug into your Mac or PC and go.

Audio-Technica's AT2035PK is a cardioid condenser with XLR connection.

Shure SM7B -You'll probably hear this mentioned as the boss of dynamic, cardioid mics and its reputation for a clear, warm signal precedes it. Their sound is revered as an industry standard, but if you're a beginner and don't want to fiddle around with XLR cables and interfaces the price point may put you off.

Samson Go – It's tiny, it's cute, it's an affordable clip-on condenser USB mic that lets you switch between cardioid and omni modes. It also has a headphone port for monitoring your vocals. It's no SM7B for sound quality but comes at a fraction of the price. As with any mic, the closer you hold it to your mouth, the stronger the vocal signal will be in contrast to the background noise picked up.

Location recording

Whilst we've touched upon a few helpful tips for getting the best sound out of a moving target, if say, you wanted to record an interview of two people walking in nature without a) getting too close or b) tripping them up with an XLR cable, you might want to look at a more professional option that includes wireless microphones with transmitters and receivers. This will allow you to transmit the signal to a recorder from a distance whilst monitoring it. They are also helpful if you're recording video at the same time as you can even throw the mixed signal onwards to your camera.

Sennheiser produce wireless kits including lavelier mics (also known as lapel mics) which clip onto clothing and deliver a good omnidirectional sound. You can also buy kit in bundles to include a belt-pack transmitter and receiver.

The Rode Wireless GO is a battery powered, omnidirectional condenser mic and transmitter in one, plus a receiver you can connect to your recording device. Apparently you can use up to 8 of them in the same location, although I've certainly never tried!

Other manufacturers are available.

Other microphone tips and accessories

At the start of your recording, don't forget to record 20 - 30 seconds of room 'tone' (essentially the sound of your room when nobody is talking or making noise) so that you or your editor can remove general room ambience in the edit if required.

If you're recording outside or on location it's not just a portable mic you'll want to consider, but some weatherproof casing as well as windsocks, muffs, fluffies and other cheeky-sounding things. These will help minimise the elements playing having with your perfect sound - although don't take that as an excuse to stand in a gale and test it. Always look for a sheltered spot if it's the voice you want to hear, rather than the weather!

Simple lapel mics will allow you to record into a mobile phone (The Rode Smartlav+ is a lapel mic adapted particularly for you Apple users) but if you're using your mobile phone jack to record, you won't be able to monitor the signal whilst it's recording unless you have wireless headphones or an extra dongle. Without monitoring your recording, any pops, rustles or gusts of wind spoiling your perfect take won't be discovered until you listen back.

Ultimately, you can spend a lot of time fiddling around with different mics for different situations which perhaps isn't the best use of your time when you're supposed to be thinking about the nature of your content. If you get bogged down, consider hiring or bringing in the professionals for a quick route to the most sophisticated equipment for the situation.

User

Remember that third element in getting a great recording sound? As you've probably realised, the position and behaviour of your guest or presenter matters, especially where microphone polarity is narrow. For cardioid and bidirectional mics, making sure you have a steady position and don't wave around too much will keep the sound even and consistent.

Making sure your guests can maintain eye contact or see scripts and prompts without having to move their head too much will help you avoid this when establishing your recording setup.

Earlier we mentioned the Promixity Effect. When a speaker or instrument is especially close to a microphone, it can emphasise the bass, especially in lower, male voices. This can be quite useful for emphasis or effect, but can also mean an inconsistent sound if your speaker isn't always in the same position. Worse still, another side effect is distortion if the speaker is too loud. One to be aware of if using bidirectional or cardioid microphones.

However, it's good practise not to be five miles away from your microphone. The closer you are to your mic, the stronger the signal you will get from your vocals as opposed to that ambient room noise, meaning a cleaner sound for your edit. Just make sure you're using a pop filter for P's or positioning your microphone so that it doesn't get a direct hit from those powerful, plosive breaths. For this reason it's vital to test and monitor your mics before and during recording. This is another reason why it can be helpful to split signals for each speaker as you can adjust their gain or volume independently.

To avoid peaking too loud (where your mic signal is too strong and the sound distorts), it's best to record your speaker at a lower rather than higher gain (in this context gain is the input level of your system, so can equate to volume). If you want to be able to hear clearly it's helpful to be able to adjust headphone monitoring level separately in your setup, rather than just cranking up the mic to disastrous effect!

We'll recap these key areas in our next section.

DIGITAL AUDIO RECORDERS

Depending on the level of technicality your chosen mic and recording setup requires, you're going to need to record your audio somewhere!

But should you use a special recording device, or can you just plug your microphone into your computer and record it straight into to your DAW (digital audio workstation) or audio programme? Well, once again this depends on how complex your production is in the first place.

Single track recording- when you just need to record one voice or input (this might also be the combined signal from one more mics)

Multitrack recording- when you want to record several different inputs as separate signals. This is useful when you have several different guests on mic.

Both of these are possible to do directly into your computer using the relevant programmes, although with multitrack recording you may need an adaptor or interface to transfer the signal from all your different inputs to the computer. If you're using a single USB mic, it's probably already got an adaptor with it, hence the simple plug and play approach.

In addition, if you're in the field or if your computer is not portable or practical in your recording situation, you may wish to consider buying a recording device that allows you to record a number of inputs. This gives you flexibility towards different kinds of connections too - from XLR inputs to wireless receivers and more.

If you prefer more flexibility, there are options that allow you to record several tracks at once, monitor and adjust their levels as well as other sound quality. You can now carry in your hand your very own mixing and mastering studio. Portable audio recorders can be tidy and handheld. They can incorporate pre-loaded sound effects and music beds enabling you to mix the whole thing on location like a live radio show.

The goal of your podcast recorder is probably not to get a perfect live band recording, but to gather a range of voices and sounds on the go. And you probably will want to edit it afterwards anyway, so let's focus on the kinds of recorders that let you capture sound in this convenient way on location. For this reason we're going to steer clear of those mysterious box-like interfaces you'll see in the studios of musicians and audio engineers. As new podcasters our focus is upon ease of use and accessibility.

The below field recorders allow you to record multiple tracks independently onto a battery-powered device, usually saving data to an SD card which you can import into your computer later, either directly via the card or using USB transfer. Initially, take a look at these manufacturers:

Zoom - this manufacturer has taken the podcasting world by storm with their handy recorders offering a range of inputs. From the H4 to H6 and H8, a range of XLR ports and additional attachment mics offer you just that number of inputs. You can also use them with wireless recording. Their digital display also incorporates the ability to mix and acts as a USB interface when plugged into your computer.

Tascam - These guys offer a robust standard in digital handheld recorders, from the little but powerful DR-05X with its USB interface and inbuilt stereo mics, through to the wifi-enabled DR-44WL. The latter includes XY condenser mics and XLR inputs, presets for different input types and an easy-to-use display. Check out the range to find one that fits your needs.

Roland - Providing a selection of high-quality recorders with built-in mics, Roland's R-26 recorder combines XLR inputs with inbuilt multi-directional stereo mics whilst other models allow mic input through jack and wireless listening and control through bluetooth.

And a special mention...

Rode Procaster / Zoom PodTrak - these mixers get a special mention. They're not a handbag accessory but they're both really decent offerings for podcasters who want to create a whole studio setup with music, SFX and multitrack recording wherever they are. You can pre-set mic settings for a regular line-up, and have all your sounds pre-loaded, meaning you can end up with a fully produced show by the time you hit the stop button on the recorder.

The others...

Once again, this list is just here to help you get started in exploring the portable recording options available to you as a beginner podcaster. Many of these recorders do the same things and compete to be the leaders in convenience, compatibility and flexibility, so you're spoilt for choice. These aren't the only brands offering recorders for a range of purposes either. Sony, Marantz and Olympus are some of the other names offering kit in this space too. If the search gets overwhelming, you could also seek advice from a professional retailer or producer. Remembering that you're not making live music is a good way to stay focussed on the specifications you actually need in your portable recorder!

RECORDING FORMATS

Your recording device may default to a particular type of file or format but you may also have the option over what kind of file you want to record and work with. Some types of audio file take up less space because the digital sound data has been squished or compressed. Lossy compression makes smaller files but sound quality isn't quite as good as the original file as a result. You can also get lossless compression, which means you don't have to compromise on sound quality. Uncompressed audio files are large because they are just a raw digital audio file of the original sound and none of the data has been compressed. The size of your file also matters when it comes to how much SD card, hard drive space or upload time is required for your files - of course you always have to balance the size and quality.

Here are some common types you may have heard, and their uses:

Mp3 - one of the most universally compatible audio file types. Although this uses lossy compression it has a small size but still a good sound quality for listening which makes it a popular choice for podcasters to work with. It also makes for speedy uploads to your cloud drive for sharing with colleagues for feedback, or your podcast distribution platform.

Mp4 - Whilst the mp3 is generally an audio only format that carries the use of ID3 tags (data about the file such as title, artist, composer etc.), the mp4 allows you to include multimedia data such as video too.

M4a or Mpeg-4 / AAC - another audio compressed lossy file format. M4a is like an mp3, only it's encoded with the AAC codec, which means tighter compression than mp3s but better quality. You'll see .aac or .m4a extensions on the end of this kind of file. The sound quality is a little better than the mp3 and it's widely supported but not as universally as the mp3.

FLAC uses lossless compression so you have a smaller file size but don't lose any data. This isn't the best choice for podcasting yet as it's not compatible with the software on some devices, including Apple.

WAV - a larger and usually uncompressed audio file. It's raw so you get great quality, but to use this on the web or for distribution across other platforms you'll need to compress it to an mp3 at the last stage. Remember to back up your original file before you do this and by all means record your elements as WAVs for best quality in the production process. AIFF is another uncompressed lossless format.

A couple more terms you might come across. Have you heard about bit rate and sample rate? These also play a part in the quality of sound on a file.

Bit rate: this means the amount of data encoded per second of audio. The higher the bit rate, the more data, thus the higher the quality. If you have a complex programme with lots of music, sounds and voices, it makes sense to encode your mp3s at a higher bit rate. 128kbps is of a good quality and typical for music and podcasts. For speech alone, a bit rate of 64kbps is alright.

Sample rate: this is how many times per second the audio tech transforms sound to data. A higher sample rate means more data per second. A typical sample rate for audio is 44.1KHz which means the audio is sampled 44100 times per second when recording and a player will build this 44100 times per second when playing. Whilst professional studios may use a higher sample rate, this is adequate for the human voice and a good standard for ease of editing and sharing.

WHAT FORMAT SHALL I EXPORT MY MP3S IN?

As mentioned, you have a simple mono speech programme you can probably get away with exporting your mp3 at a lower bitrate such as 64kbps. However this doesn't really provide an adequate standard of sound quality if you have anything more complex in your programme. Therefore for the sake of having one less thing to consider, exporting your stereo mp3 at no lower than 128kbps should mean you don't compromise the quality of music for most listeners and don't significantly increase the time it takes for them to download the file.

WHEN DOES QUALITY MATTER MOST?

To paraphrase Coco Chanel, mix shabbily and they remember the mix; mix impeccably and they remember the podcast.

However, we've outlined why impeccable sound is actually pretty difficult to achieve in every situation, and it is down to many factors.

Although it makes the sound editor in me uneasy to say this, with regards podcasting, I'd suggest aiming for the best quality you can achieve without losing sight of the main goal: a comfortable and physically easy listening experience.

You could spend plenty of time learning about audio file formats and their nuances. However, the most audible parts of your programme are established with great recording techniques and a quality edit and mix in the first place. Disparities in sound quality are more likely to stand out to your average podcast listener than the finer frequency difference between a quality mp3 and M4a! In fact, if people are listening on a standard pair of headphones they picked up from a mass-market retailer, they probably won't be able to hear the difference anyway.

DIY EDITING

So you want to have a go at this yourself. OK! Editing programmes are used not just for chopping up and building your programme, but for treating the tracks you've recorded, removing problems, fixing volumes and boosting or reducing certain qualities of the sound. They're also the place where you pull your programme together and export it to your chosen file format. You can even use them for recording into in the first place.

You might optionally want to experiment with some of the capabilities your software has to adjust things like frequency, dynamic compression and room effects like reverb. This can be a highly specialised job as there is much to learn through exploration of sound engineering principles. However, that's beyond the remit of a beginner and indeed this book! Do have a play around with the tools and their presets if this interests you though. Many plugins are very user-friendly and have presets to manipulate sounds much like the filters on your Instagram photos. The order or 'chain' in which you deploy them also makes a difference too. When hiring a professional mixer or editor this is the specialised sort of knowledge they can bring to your process.

However, unless you're composing music, fixing problems or creating wonderfully complex soundscapes, you can get started in podcasting without this sort of knowledge. If it's an interview you're editing, you're better off focussing on making sure you don't clip breaths half way through and making sure the pacing of the language is right after you've chopped out the ummms, aaahs, errrrrs, etc.

As we've said before, you can minimise the need for sound manipulation in the mixing process if you've recorded in a good environment on a half decent microphone in the first place.

There are a myriad of audio editing programmes available to you, (not to mention noise-reduction tools to mitigate mistakes or problems!) these days. You can even get most of them without having to buy extra kit, although at the very least you might want to invest in some good quality headphones. Gone are the days of cutting bits of tape together at just the right moment. Pretty much every mistake you make in editing is reversible (just never forget to copy and back up your original files!).

Different programmes are designed for different purposes. Some are more suitable for professionals editing music and doing complex things with tempo, MIDI or plugged-in instruments, whereas others are geared to simple chopping around. Some allow you to change the keyboard shortcuts to match functions of other, similar programmes and speed up your process. Some are built to integrate video and are used widely in TV, music or video editing too.

For a beginner editing podcasts, most basic DAWs (Digital Audio Workstations) will allow you to do what you need to do, that is: editing clips, adjusting volumes, removing unwanted noises, mixing and exporting files. Beyond that are the more professional features that come with more sophisticated programmes.

If you're keen to try out different editing programmes, many offer you free or limited-time trials or even month-to-month subscriptions so you can explore what best suits your needs and importantly, what you most enjoy working on. Here are 6 common DAWs which you may encounter. These are by no means the only ones on the market:

Audacity- A free, open-source, multi-track editor that's beginner-friendly.

GarageBand - Apple's DAW comes installed on mac with a library of loops and sound-effects you can use without worrying about copyright. You can record into your Apple device, add artwork and so on. It's beginner friendly.

Reaper - Recording, editing, mixing, multitrack. It's capable of the lot without being too expensive.

Adobe Audition - A commonly used professional software for podcasting and audio programmes. It allows you to use multi-track and single track edit views, you can incorporate plugins, play around with time and tempo and deliver sophisticated mixes. In spite of these professional features it's pretty easy for beginners to pick up and you can adjust your keyboard shortcuts too, which I personally find helpful for speed.

Pro Tools - A multitrack editor and music production programme with professional features. Having started in radio imaging this is my personal DAW of choice. There's a free version you can try out to make up your own mind.

Logic Pro X - Another editor for sophisticated sound and music production, this Apple programme is the professional evolution of Garageband with more features.

Like learning any new skill, this is not something you can become amazing at overnight. The best way to learn to edit is by editing... and by making mistakes. Practise makes perfect. The process may be slow and frustrating at first, but the more you practise, the faster and more intuitive it becomes and the more confident you will become. Plus you'll get a real kick out of finishing your episode!

In the beginning this may feel like learning to drive a car without an instructor: You live in fear that you will cause irrevocable damage at any turn. But unlike learning to drive without an instructor, you probably won't. This is where it's useful if you have a friend you can call up if you get stuck. Even the swiftest, most experienced editors find it a grind to switch programmes when they're used to using one more than another. Because using your programme, much like the skill of editing itself, becomes intuitive over time.

In the same way you wouldn't expect a professional editor to learn your job in day, nor can you master theirs in the same timeframe, so do make sure you are prepared to invest time in learning the ropes, or giving your chosen staff-member scope to do this if you're going down the DIY route.

However if you want a kick-start, you might consider doing a short course, looking at YouTube tutorials, or hiring a teacher to give you some sessions. These resources will not only help you discover things you never knew about the programmes but will help you find smarter ways of using them.

GIVE YOUR EARS A BREAK

This isn't a book about how to edit, but if you are DIYing it, please take this one piece of advice: however fantastic something sounds after 10 hours at your keyboard, walk away and come back to it when your body and mind have had a good rest. Have you ever looked at a picture hanging in your house day after day until you just don't notice it any more? This happens even if you absolutely love that picture. We are adapted to develop a blind spot to things that we are part of our regular environment and for this reason your ear may become accustomed to a glaringly bad edit after a hard day's listening. Your ears will burn out after a few hours so take regular breaks and never put something out without having a listen through! You'll thank me for this small but fundamental piece of advice!

WHAT TO CONSIDER WHEN BUYING HEADPHONES?

And speaking of ears!

In the days of home or desk editing, it's not always convenient (or affordable) to build a studio with high-end monitors for mixing. Headphones present a simple solution to delivering edits in a variety of locations and allowing you to get a well-balanced mix whilst blocking out distracting room noises.

There are various reasons why your typical high-street headphones and earbuds might not be the best choice for professional podcast work. Firstly, they can be designed to emphasise certain frequencies, perhaps bassier for music. Or they might be small, cheap and tinny-sounding. Either way, cheap headphones can make for a lower quality sound. On the other hand even if you've got yourself a fancy pair of noise-cancelling headphones their manipulation of the sound might give an untrue representation of what your audio is truly like too!

Choosing a pair of headphones for podcast production will be influenced by how you want to use them. Rather than earbuds, let's look at the kinds that cover your ears:

Headphones which have a closed cup mean sound doesn't leak out so easily. You can isolate sounds and cut off the distractions of the outside world! For this reason these closed-back kinds are helpful for use when recording audio and quality control, as you don't get the sound bleeding through to be picked up by microphones.

Although not essential, open-back headphones are a premium choice for editing and mixing your programmes. By letting in room and background sounds, you can get a more natural feel for the live environment in which your audio will actually be consumed. And as people tend to listen to podcasts whilst they're doing other things, this can be an important consideration for your sound. Of course, if you're editing in a busy office or noisy environment, there can be drawbacks to letting the world in!

The more sensitive and wide the frequency response of a headphone, the better you will be able to make out and balance the sounds in your mix. If you are combining music, vocals, and different sounds, you'll want to hear them all as true and clear as they are so you can adjust everything sit at just the right level in the mix. Bear in mind of course, that whatever the capacity of your headphones, everyone's ears are different, and the average range of human hearing is between 20Hz and 20KHz. This does vary with age, experience and other factors just as your eyesight does.

Another important consideration is how comfortable over-ear headphones feel when draped over your head for hours on end. Trying different types for their weight and headband tightness before you buy is a smart move. Nobody likes sore ear cartilage at the end of a long day's work.

Even after balancing the mix using a quality pair of headphones, I find it useful to check a final mix on a variety of different kinds of high-street headphones, so that I can have a closer feel for what it will be like when listeners download it on their phone podcast app and listen through their earbuds.

PART 4 - SHOW PREPARATION AND RECORDING

- **Structure**
- **Pre-planning interviews**
- **Editing for story**
- **The presenter's role**
- **Recording: How to prepare for anything**

Now that you have your show concept, your kit and your chosen presenter all lined up and ready to go, there is one more thing that you need to do before you can start recording: you should develop a plan for the day.

You COULD race headlong into your very first interview or conversation, then worry about how to piece it all together later. This is one approach indeed, but by making sure you have a plan in place before you get on mic, you're more likely to make the most of your time behind the mic, to get what you're looking for and to have space to respond to anything unexpected. The unexpected might take the form of your batteries failing, someone turning up late, or your guest giving you an surprising exclusive that you need extra time for. Whatever it is, some careful preparation will help you stay cool, on track and will make sure you achieve what you want with the time available. As my father says: "If you don't know where you are going, all roads lead there"!

Creating a template through which to plan each show and script bits in advance can give you a ready-made structure to adapt to any guest or interview. The benefit of this is to give you a feel for approximate timings, so that you can keep in mind what the edited product will sound like and how much time you have to really get to the crux of things with your guest. It will also help you focus your line of questioning on what matters most. It's always nice to have some relaxing chat and some warm-up time with a guest, but not at the expense of your all-important questions. At the same time, if you make sure you cover your basic points by thinking them through ahead of time, you allow space for unplanned and interesting things to happen too. An interview rarely shakes down exactly the way you planned it, but if you plan carefully, you can create a the right environment to cover what you need, build rapport and make your guest comfortable enough to share more of themselves than you expected.

WHY FOCUS MATTERS

When you come to the edit, it pays to be insecure. Think of a ticking clock from the moment the edited programme starts: With every second that passes the listener is more likely to lose interest, become distracted by social media, or break off for a conversation with someone in the same room. You're vying for the attention of someone who is really very important and busy, but whom for some reason has chosen to give you the benefit of the doubt because they think you might have something useful to offer. Get to the point, keep them interested and use all your powers of persuasion to show them why this topic should matter to them. It's true that podcast users aren't as flighty as those engaging with some other communications mediums. They are curious people who invest a lot of time and attention on the programmes they select. They aren't looking for noise for the sake of it and they've chosen you because they think you have something to offer. The worst thing you could do is disappoint them and waste their time!

This outlook begins at the planning and recording phase, because the structure you plan for your show will be successful only if you have recorded everything you need in the first place. This means considering what the narrative constituents of your story might be.

LINEAR STRUCTURE

Even if you're doing a straightforward interview show, it's worth thinking about your beginning, middle and end because you still need to raise interesting questions and answer them. In a linear structure this might break down something like this, for example (not a rule though):

Introduction: Explain what your show is about and its intriguing benefits. If you are keen to explain the connection to your business here keep it brief: Your aim is to respect the listener's valuable time and get into the episode topic as quickly as possible. Your listener has not tuned in for an advert, they've tuned in because they want to find out more about the topic of the episode.

96

Beginning: Presenter or narrator sets out the who, when, where, why and how of the programme. What is the problem, what are we going to find out in this episode and why does it matter now? What's more, why should the listener care? Again, this might be very brief, or it may need some background context and storytelling to get to the heart of the issue. Bear in mind that there are creative ways you can illustrate this and tease the content ahead with clips, music, or drama to break up your presenter's narration. Quickly meet the guest or guests, establish their credentials and why they will be interesting to listen to.

Middle (the longest bit): Hopefully you got here and got your listener hooked into the big question before they switched off and put on their favourite Michael Jackson album instead. Move through your discussion or questions here, increasing the complexity of the topic so that the need-to-know basics are established first, and you can build on each new piece of information with a new question. The amount of prior knowledge you will assume on the part of your audience may vary but you may want to lay down the basics first. In an interview situation, try to give examples of abstract topics in context so that ideas can come to life through stories. Giving your audience something to visualise and emotionally connect with will mean these ideas remain with them and mean something. They are also more likely to retain information if it is told as a story. It also makes it a lot more interesting to listen to!

End: Presenter sums up the learnings, does final thoughts from guests and looks at how what we've learned can be applied in new ways or places. Perhaps leave the listener with a powerful emotional image that contextualises the conversation and gives them something to think about. You might also want to direct them to further reading, information or support based on the subject matter.

Outro: Short and sweet. This is where you might want to solicit for feedback or interaction on social media and maybe tell the listener a little something more about your business, now you've earned their respect! Try and keep this to as few 'calls to action' as possible so it doesn't end up being longer than the rest of the episode. This is also your final port of call to send your listener to the next step in your marketing funnel, so if you want to drive them to sign up to something or visit a website you can include that here too. You don't have to record this with your guest in the room unless you want them to share some links themselves. Remember not to bombard listeners with too many actions though. Stating one clear call to action and directing people to show notes for more information on other matters is much clearer and will save time too.

CONVERSATIONS ARE MESSY

The overview described above shows you the FINAL EDIT of how an interview might be structured in a linear fashion, but the original interview itself will likely be far from orderly - it's a dynamic conversation after all!

Having a pre-planned idea of topics you'd like to cover in the meaty middle section not only means you will remember to prioritise these points but will also give you confidence and direction so you can make the most of your time with the guest or guests. Bullet-pointing these in a flexible order, rather than reading out pre-written questions, will allow you or your presenter to deliver them in a way that is not disruptive to the natural flow of the conversation.

You might also want to share a summary of talking points with your guests beforehand so they can think about the topics they'd like to cover. Do beware of being too 'scripted' in this approach though, as it might entice wooden-sounding pre-prepared responses from your guests.

MORE COMPLEX STRUCTURES

If your planned programme will be anything more complex than a series of linear conversations, you'll likely be recording several interviews and piecing together a final, connecting narrative afterwards. For that reason it's even more important to plan your interview points well and leave extra time for the surprise topics and titbits that arise and offer that little something extra to your wider story. These may end up changing the slant of your whole episode!

If you are including many contributors in an episode it worth researching and bullet-pointing your whole show before you do your final recorded interviews. Conducting telephone or face to face pre-interviews - if you can get time with contributors - will help you get a clearer picture of the issues, quirks and stance of each guest too.

In advance of recording, work out the questions you'd like answered from each interview as well as the general information you'd like them to convey and brief guests as appropriate. With any luck you'll gain more insight than you bargained for. Although you may not use it all in the final programme, it will give you flexibility to chop things around later.

Your pre-research will allow you to be ready with questions that separate interviews might raise for one another. This will come in handy if you want to bin a linear structure and play around in the edit later on, making conflicts or concurrences even clearer.

EDITING FOR STORY AND SUSPENSE

If you are looking to compile an intricate and unfolding tale with intrigue, surprises, twists and turns, this is a sophisticated skill and planning will be essential. The questions you, your contributors or narrator raise will guide the listener's attention and the direction of narrative. The details you hold back in a suspenseful production are also just as important as those that you reveal, as their absence creates questions and causes the listener to participate by thinking for themselves.

At the editing stage there are no rules, there is just good storytelling! You can play around with the order in which you present your recorded content to create suspense and intrigue, or to focus on side-topics as you build up to a bigger picture. Each piece of audio should add complexity, clarity or interest to what has come before, in order to drive the story forwards.

Once all the interviews are gathered, you can re-order and write the narrated sections of your programme to build the story in an interesting way, perhaps drip-feeding the facts and keeping some revelations back for later.

At this point, a transcription service, or an automated transcription software such as Trint or Descript can save you loads of time by timecoding the spoken text for easy editing later. Depending on how your mind works, you might like to add notes on scraps of paper, digitally map, annotate, or even print, snip and physically re-order sections of text on a corkboard (old-school but whatever works for you!). Either way, it's great fun working out how to present bits of story before writing those all-important bits of connective prose! Hopefully a this pre-edit or 'paper' edit process will help you resolve issues with pace, information and structure before you've got down to the actual edit. I prefer a well-planned audio edit as this frees up headspace to focus on making sure it sounds really smooth. It also allows more time for the creative use of sound, music and sound effects. These adjustments can make a big impact on your finished product if your programme requires it.

As you're probably starting to realise, I'm a big fan of planning ahead in order that you may have scope to diverge and get creative when it matters!

This might be overkill for many, but when you REALLY get into thinking about narrative structure, you might want to plot out your episodes themselves as steps along the way to a whole series narrative. Building structure on a micro and macro scale might seem like a highly-complex thing to pre-plan and adapt to, but there are many interesting theory books on this. However human beings do seem to have a natural born instinct for unfolding a tale. Whether that's because we are read similar fables and fairytales as children, the same classics as adults, or just simply because there is something universal in keeping other people interested in what we have to say, we are natural storytellers. Everything starts with a question or problem to resolve, a conflict to overcome, a journey to go on and some interesting people to clash, grow and know.

Giving each interview or feature a purpose in the narrative is a good criteria to help you decide what to leave on the cutting room floor. Everything you leave in the final edit should move the questions or learnings of your listener forwards. This principle is the same whether you are making a series of interviews about gardening's impact on mental health or a 6-part drama about a real-life property scandal.

- If every interview gives you a useful piece of knowledge, how does it inform the message of the episode?
- And optionally, if every episode leaves you with an idea or piece of knowledge, how does that inform the message or unfolding of the whole series?

SMART INTERVIEWS, PLENTY OF SCOPE

To recap, then, an easy way to build a complicated narrative is to plan and research your interviews to make sure they include all the key information you need with scope for a few surprises.

Then afterwards, you can rationalise the information from all your contributors into a paper edit and write the connecting elements that tie it all together as a story.

Continuing to deepen the listener's understanding and intrigue with your subject matter is the name of the game and there is no limit on how you use the interviews or content you have gathered to do this. The peak of the narrative and excitement may take the form of a revelation or it may be the missing piece of the puzzle. Either way, after this point there is a natural transition to tying up loose ends and bringing it all together in your conclusion. This may be spurred by a late revelation that brings it all together, or a general bringing-together of what the episode has taught us.

For example:

Beginning: In part one we hear an issue or story that catches our attention. This might be created as an interview or a narrative piece. It might be dramatised or it might be a reading, or a combination of all of those things. Ultimately the treatment here acts as the galvanising force to begin the story and raise the core questions for your programme.

Middle: One question leads to another and things get more exciting and more intriguing. The interviews or features in the middle of the programme will deepen the story, each either posing a new question or moving the understanding and intrigue of the audience forward. You may present a revelation that changes the line of thought or questioning at some point in this section. This might take you off on a side-alley with even smaller story arcs within it, each providing a new piece of information or a question to drive the narrative forward.

End: This where you can bring together all the questions, learnings and insights from across the episode to resolve the original question. You might return to interviews from earlier in the episode or series. You might also reflect upon the issues that aren't yet resolved and how they relate to the contexts. Leaving your listener with a deeper understanding of the topic in their world as well as something to reflect on over their day or discuss with friends makes for a satisfying end to any time investment they've made with you!

With regards timing, in the example above, the middle is the meat of the story and as with any book, film or radio show will take up the bulk of the content. For a 30-minute programme, you might be looking at 3 or 4 minutes for the beginning and end, with the middle taking up the other 24-22 minutes. That's not a precise rule, of course, but useful for planning your edit. How your programme sounds in the final edit will come down to your instinct and feeling for its rhythm. And as we've said before, it may be different to your original plotting sheet, depending on where your recordings take you. Ultimately having a plan just means you have a direction of travel with room to adapt along the way.

THE PRESENTER'S ROLE

The presenter's role depends very much upon your listener, the guests and the style of programme you are creating.

Perhaps you are building the whole thing yourself and just bringing in the presenter as a narrator. If that's the case, you'd hope at the very least they can have some editorial input into the script to reflect their own stance and style.

If they are charged with conducting the interviews and posing all of your questions, the presenter's role in such an environment is not simply to ask the questions you've planned out, but to interact with the guest's points, to ask them to elaborate or explain, and in some cases to add depth to the conversation by sharing their own experiences or recap to the listener any factual learnings in simple terms. A presenter taking the subject and making it their own is the best you can hope for, because it makes the difference between a sincere interrogation of your subject and a paid performance. Listeners can sniff out the latter a mile off and might find it unappealing.

If you are going for a conversational show, it's essential to shift the balance of power so that the presenter and guest can connect on the same level. Put everyone at their ease, brief them on the plan and allow everyone time to ask questions beforehand.

If you are going for a factual, interview show, it's still essential that the presenter can build a personal rapport with the guest, but they will need to assume the level of understanding of a listener, and if that means they aren't an expert in the subject, they need to ask the basic questions and assume no prior knowledge. Just because you pre-brief them effectively on all that brilliant research you've done, it doesn't mean the listener will have been. Arming the presenter with this knowledge is generally there to help them extract it from their guests, not to deliver it as the voice of god! It's far more interesting for listeners to learn alongside the presenter, rather than be lectured to.

In short, you need to decide whether your listener will be a fly on the wall to a personal conversation, or the implicit force behind the presenter's interview questions.

WHEN RECORDING GOES WRONG

Technology and changing circumstances can present new challenges in every recording. When you're backed into a corner, sometimes it's helpful to have a quick fix to hand, so what follows is a list of common problems and some solutions or preventions to reduce the risk of them distracting you from the matter in hand. As you become more confident with your kit and productions, perhaps you'll even start to enjoy the problem-solving(!)

One tactic for the risk averse is this: bring a spare everything. That goes for batteries, SD cards, cables, microphones, even your recording device if you have a spare. Unfortunately there is no backup for a celeb presenter that decides to have a meltdown, you're just going to have to do an on-the-spot repair job on that one. But for everything else, having a spare is a good quick fix when you're in the middle of a recording situation.

My second piece of advice is to always wear headphones when you are recording! Being able to monitor the signal coming through the microphone will allow you to spot problems as they happen and not find out afterwards when there might be nothing you can do about it! If you can hear a crackly cable, a dodgy microphone, or the 16:53 to Alicante zooming overhead as it's happening, you have a chance to fix the problem or re-record something on the spot.

Scenario: A global pandemic causes everyone to be confined to their homes and / or social distancing rules enforced.
Solution: Once upon a time it was all about having an ISDN studio for a quality 'down the line' sound, but now plenty of ordinary people have a means of recording an okay-sounding signal without. As we all learned in 2020, the internet enables us to adapt at extraordinary pace. Even with just a wifi link you can record a low-quality "in person" interview remotely, but given that a vast number of people walk around with smartphones in their pockets (AKA mobile microphones), a great option is to brief them on how to use their voice memos app to record themselves, then show them where and how close to hold the mic and make sure they're in a quiet, softly-furnished room. Then all you need is an interface for your conversation. Get guests to plug their headphones into a computer and join a video conferencing call so that you can see each other (you can also record this audio as a backup to the cloud or your computer) and you have one fairly decent

solution. Other options might be to use online conferencing services that record the local signal in higher quality, or to courier your guest a microphone and recorder. You can only mitigate to a certain degree operator technique and environment from afar, so don't expect perfection.

Every day there seem to be more online programmes or apps coming to market to make remote recording easier and the quality better. Current examples of this sort of application include MicDropp, SquadCast, Zencastr and Cleanfeed to name a few. Depending on your needs, some of these options will record files and save them to a cloud for you, others will allow you mix whole shows and export your recording as one file. Don't forget to check they are compatible with the relevant devices ahead of recording though.

The option you choose for remote recording will be a balance between the technical expertise of your participants and your need for a good recording quality. Don't assume guests are all technically adept and check that they own smartphones before planning your approach. If you end up walking someone through a process they've never tried, it may be time-consuming, but on the plus side you will have shared a useful new skill with them and converted another person to team-tech savvy!

Scenario: Your recorder has run out of batteries
Solution: Hopefully you brought some spare batteries. If you didn't, reach for the smartphone. You can even get microphones that plug into mobile phone headphone jacks. I usually carry a Rode Smartlav+ lapel mic which is very portable. For its tiny size it certainly frees up a lot of space in the mental worry bank.

Scenario: It's raining cats and dogs
Solution: Don't get your kit wet. It's electrical stuff. Speaking as someone who spends a lot of time outside in the rain, it's not worth the worry. What if you get back and you've lost everything?! Check the forecast when you're planning recordings, invest in some decent waterproof carrying equipment for your kit - improvise if you have to - carry a towel and those little silica bags around in your kit bag and take a brolly or two (although you will pick up rain sounds if you're holding it over your mic) - even someone to hold them. Whilst you're at it why not gear yourself up from top to bottom too. There's no point having a dry kit if your hands are too cold or drippy to operate it. The

day I gave up looking trendy and ordered some proper farming workwear for my outdoor recordings was a happy one indeed. Water can be a challenge: I remember recording in a waterpark once where we put condoms over microphones to protect them from unwanted splashes. In another situation our daring presenter smuggled a GoPro in its waterproof case down a very long waterslide. The audio was muffled but worth it for the sheer stupidness of hearing them wailing their way down to the bottom. Don't do this sort of thing without a permission and proper health and safety and risk assessment though, obviously.

Scenario: The wind up here is ridiculous
Solution: What? I can't hear you over the wind! Powerful wind can cause your microphone to rumble and ruin your recording. Omni mics can generally handle a little more wind-beating, but what to do when your everyday mic won't cut it in the elements? Step 1) Find shelter, whether indoors, behind a break, or by using your own body and clothing. Facing your mic directly into the force of the gale isn't the smartest choice of position. Step 2) If still needed, roll out some specialist equipment to reduce the amount of vibration on your mic. Hopefully you have a basic windshield with your mic in the first instance. These foam covers snuggle around the mic capsule and absorb some of the wind energy. Have you heard of a deadcat though? These fluffy, furry shields are the next level up and allow extra protection without muffling the sound too much. An omni microphone with a windshield will give you the best chance of a good sound in wind.

On occasions where you need to use a shotgun microphone in the wind, perhaps even on a boompole, let's hope you've been doing your push-ups and are ready for the upper body workout. These sensitive and directional mics have yet another solution. Blimps and Zepplins are the next step up from a windcover and dead cat, providing the best of both in one Zeppelin-shaped enclosure.

With any rumble-reducing covers you still might need to emphasise or reduce certain frequencies in post-production to get the best sound.

Scenario: It's so cold my cables have frozen and snapped.
Solution: This is where it's useful to have a really cool engineer friend, because if you're recording in freezing wind or icy conditions this can be a real concern. Fortunately there are loads of extreme

environment-dwelling sound people who are happy to share their tips and tricks on blogs, so you can do a bit of research before you even head outside. Brittle cables, frozen kit and battery life are worries when things get super cold so keeping your kit and cables as close to normal temperatures as possible is the goal. Take a fresh memory card for each day, and take lots of spare batteries. Wrap them in every layer you can. A sock might make for a more muffled sounding mic but it will help ease the wind factor. Keep everything in lightweight, weatherproof kit and use silica packs to stop water ingress and subsequent freezing. Your body is a good little heat source so keep kit close to your body and wear it inside your coat. As for microphones, experiment with where your presenter can wear this - perhaps under their chin, inside their coat, or up in a mask if they are wearing one. You'll need to be careful of clothes rustling so will probably need to take along some fluffies to protect the mic from that too. If you can, test, test, test before the big day. It might also help to take woven rather than rubber cables.

Scenario: My recorder is behaving really weirdly and I don't think it's recording.
Solution: I'd always advise taking the time to troubleshoot and correct the original problem if you can. As a producer you can get used to putting everyone else's needs first. If you get a tech problem like this, it's easy to feel pressured by time constraints or fidgety presenters to stop holding things up and to just hope for the best, but that's no good if you end up with missing or damaged audio! Always take five and have a play around with the kit to find out what the problem is. If it's not resolvable, this is where you whip out your backup recorder. Even if it's not as great quality or doesn't allow you to use your fancy mics, a mobile phone, or online cloud recording for backup is always a load off your mind, especially in fraught or fast-moving situations.

Scenario: I've pressed something and now I can't figure out what it's doing.
Solution: As above, take the time to figure it out. You need only work this one out once and you'll be ready for it again. When I got my first Zoom H6 Multitrack recorder and was recording a live sitcom with an audience, I managed to pair the mics as stereo tracks during the session and it took a little nerve-wracking time to work out how to unpair them. The lesson there is that it's always worth a quick read of the manual before using a new piece of equipment! If you have a

problem that isn't covered in the manual I recommended hitting the forums. You are rarely the first person to have a problem and the internet is full of helpful questions and answers.

Scenario: My recorder isn't registering a sound signal.
Solution: This is where you want to be nice and logical. Don't assume it's your recorder that's causing the problem. If it all looks good, you've got the channel open, the volume is up, your headphones and mic plugged in.... then you want to systematically investigate your headphones, your cable and your microphone one at a time, swapping them with others to see if that fixes the problem. Follow the chain piece by piece to work out where the weak link lies.

Scenario: We have a no-show.
Solution: You have a guest standing in front of you who has a very tight timetable. Your presenter hasn't turned up and they're not answering the phone. What do you do? Well, the beauty of podcasting, as opposed to live radio, is that your listeners aren't sitting there waiting at that very moment. You have an embarrassment of options. Firstly, mistakes happen, so your guest might well accept that your presenter has been delayed somewhere and agree to wait or reschedule. If that's not possible, you might have to step into the breach and take the interview yourself. If it's not going to fit your format to have a random interviewer on mic, make sure you don't cross-talk so you can chop out your questions afterwards and re-record them with your presenter later. Alternatively, ask your guest to answer in full sentences so that you can edit this together as a full narrative piece afterwards and just drop it into the show. Problem solved! If, however, the problem is a lack of guest and it's your presenter who is ready and waiting and on a tight schedule, see if you can get that guest on a video call for the interview, or even on the phone. Yes, the phone. People will still listen to phone calls if the person speaking is worth listening to.

Scenario: Popping P's and plosives
Solution: If your P's or any other breath sound is creating a distortion on the mic, it's because the power of the sound is causing your mic diaphragm to vibrate heavily. The closer the speaker is, the more powerful the impact of these plosives, and because of the proximity effect, the more noticeable this low frequency bang or pop sounds. This can be difficult to fix in post-production. In the first place, try and avoid this happening by making sure your guest isn't too close to the

mic. If this doesn't solve it, make sure they are not blowing straight into the capsule. As with wind or any other high-energy sound source, the more sensitive and directional the mic, the greater the vibration it will pick up. You could try re-angling the mic just below their mouth, rather than in front of it, so it's not in the immediate line of fire. However, even the best mic etiquette still often needs some extra help. That's why you can buy (or make) something called a pop filter or pop shield. This is just a perforated surface that sits a couple of inches in front of the mic, dissipating the blast of air so that where high frequencies can pass through, lower frequencies have less power. Pop filters / shields are commonly used in the studio.

Scenario: What's that rumbling?
Solution: In the studio, your energetic guest keeps smacking their hand on the desk for emphasis, or they're tapping their foot under the table and shaking the whole thing. Step one is to ask them to cut it out right now, albeit gently. However they're probably not doing this consciously or on purpose and thus might just do it again anyway, if you haven't already made them too self-conscious to talk. With sensitive studio microphones, mechanical vibration of the apparatus can be a problem, so it's worth thinking about a shock mount. These devices attach to a boom arm or mic stand and suspend your mic elastically, meaning that if the desk and mic stand picks up mechanical noise, your mic doesn't have to.

In the field, handling noise can also be an issue, if your avid reporter is gleefully massaging the microphone shaft, leaning on or twiddling the cable, your mic might just pick up on the vibration and make for unwelcome sounds. In this scenario, as in the studio, you have another example of why it's crucial to monitor the recording with headphones so that you can hear and resolve issues on the spot. If you're in the field and these problems are unavoidable, perhaps consider whether you're equipped with the best mic for the occasion. An omnidirectional mic, lapel or shotgun might all present a better alternative.

Scenario: My presenter is being "difficult".
Solution: Bad behaviour normally means that there is a problem to be solved. Give them a few minutes to regain their composure and ask if you can do anything to make things easier. Your presenter is the one 'out front' and if they feel out of their depth, underprepared or stressed by some other factor there's nowhere for them to hide. It's

your job as a producer to create the best environment and provide the means for them to bring good energy and do their job well. You might not be able to fix all the issues, but getting grumpy with them will not help the immediate situation either. Support your presenter as best you can and put your own feelings aside in the moment. There is nothing more vulnerable than being filmed or recorded when you're stressed, struggling for words or not at your best. Even if you can't solve a problem, you can make sure they have space and dignity to get themselves together and jump back on it.

Scenario: One of my mics isn't working.
Solution: Double, double check you have the recording channel open on your device. If it's definitely your mic, swap it out for a spare. Even if it's not the same kind of microphone, perhaps your recorder comes with a built-in option or XY attachment you could plug in and use. If you don't have a spare available, not even a phone or lapel, then that's pretty annoying. It's great to have one clean signal for each guest. However, if you have just one mic available, consider which type it is. Does it have the option to record in a bidirectional mode? Great, problem solved. If it's a handheld omnidirectional model you could get your presenter to take turns with the guest like they do in Vox pops on the news, or just hold it in between them at a decent proximity. If your presenter and guest have to share, microphone position is everything in getting a good sound. If it's your standard cardioid, then consider the narrow sound field; make sure you get both speakers within the best possible proximity and instruct them on where to direct their voice. Taking turns at an awkward angle sure won't make for the most chilled out interview, but if you have no other option it might just get you something. If you've more than one guest in a room, its probably best to make the people with the least to say to one another share a mic so off-mic cross-talking and awkward pauses aren't a problem.

Scenario: SD card problems.
Solution: Don't buy cheap SD cards! All sorts of weirdness can happen with them. I've noticed that changing the batteries mid-way through recording can cause some strange formatting issues and hair-raising moments. This is one fantastic reason to make sure your batteries are fully charged ahead of any recording and even have a backup recording running. Even with a good SD card, I always format them ahead of a fresh recording and test it (but make sure you've got any files you want off it first as this process will wipe the data).

Scenario: This room has high levels of background noise.

Solution: This comes down to finding a decent recording environment in the first place. If you're stuck with the world's least helpful room, get your speaker as close to the mic as you can without causing sound problems. This will mean the signal you get from them is stronger in comparison to the background noise. Also make sure you record 20-30 seconds of room tone - this is essentially just the sound of the room without anyone speaking or making noises. Editing software often includes noise reduction plugins and you can also buy specialist software to help you remove specific frequencies of noise. For a handy post-production fix I recommend Izotope's RX software which includes some fantastic tools to isolate and repair sounds and reflections without the need for a degree in sound engineering.

PART 5 - HOSTING AND DISTRIBUTION

- **RSS feeds**
- **Choosing a host provider**
- **How to set up, manage and distribute your podcast**

Once you've made a thing of absolute beauty, you'll definitely want people to be able to listen to it. You've done the hard work, but perhaps you're foxed by the magic that takes this piece of audio to the ears of a listener. With so many different platforms and options out there, who can blame you? But really this is pretty straightforward and you don't need to understand code or the nuances of an RSS feed. To help with this understanding I'm going to define a few terms:

WHAT'S AN RSS FEED?

RSS stands for "really simple syndication". An RSS feed is a feed of web data that's bundled up and holds information for your programme (the audio, the text for the description, the 'metadata', or data about data, artwork etc.) and can be updated any time.

RSS feeds are used to distribute information widely as this code can be shared and read by various programmes. Programmes that read RSS feeds will be able to refresh and gather new information as it's released. These can be called RSS readers or aggregators. They basically check the feed for updates when told to, either automatically or on demand.

RSS isn't just used for sharing podcast audio, it's used for blogs, audio, video and in many news formats. When you subscribe to an RSS feed, the programme you use to read it automatically updates. That means your podcast app will automatically check for new episodes when you hit the subscribe button. And that's why everyone always asks you to subscribe at the end of their podcast - it makes a big difference to their regular numbers if you can listen to your favourite programme as soon as its available.

In the case of a podcast your RSS feed is populated with your podcast programmes, their data and their metadata. You might

112

manage this through your hosting platform and then manually share the RSS feed to an interface like Apple podcasts which then makes it available even more widely. THEN various other programmes might even pull the information through from Apple podcasts on their own platforms. All this adds up to your podcast being available in lots of places, but the original RSS feed is managed and updated through your hosting platform.

A side note here, you don't HAVE to use a bespoke hosting platform to create your RSS feed. There are sites that will allow you generate a feed if you wish to house this on your website and use that as the host. Wordpress also has a plugin to allow you to host podcasts. But it's not recommended to just upload podcasts to your website and host from there, because files can take up a lot of space and it may cause you some bandwidth problems. You might end up paying more to your web service provider to mitigate this. In that case it just be more sensible to go with a hosting provider that is designed to make a straightforward, user-friendly experience and has customer service available to help troubleshoot problems.

WHAT IS A HOSTING PLATFORM?

Talking about podcast hosting can get confusing... here, we're not talking about the beloved presenter of your show though.

Your hosting platform is simply the place your podcast RSS feed lives and is managed from. It's where you store your audio files for delivery to RSS feeds on demand. There are loads of different hosting platforms and they are all vying to offer you the edge for your money. Ultimately they are using similar technology and working with the same international rules for data and information. In the most basic sense a platform will allow you to upload files, add information and distribute episodes via and RSS feed. You will probably also be able to see to some data from that RSS feed's interactions. But there are many more features to be enjoyed, depending on your provider! Here are some of the things a hosting platform may do:

- Provide a user-friendly interface through which to manage, schedule and release podcast episodes.
- Allow you to enter and update metadata, descriptions, author information, tags and artwork.

- Allow you to add other information, such as whether the episode contains explicit content and needs to be marked as such.
- Allow you to create embeddable players for websites and social media.
- Integrate with other platforms such as Spotify, Amazon Music and YouTube.
- Permit multiple team members to manage your show.
- Integrate with platforms such as SteadyHQ to allow you to build membership or put content behind hard or soft paywalls.
- Give you access to some data on listening numbers and location as an aggregate, or even listen-through rates and the kind of device used to listen (i.e. no individual information). They might charge more for more in-depth analytics.
- Some platforms may try to offer further insights based on listeners which have listened via their platforms and consented to the sharing of this personal data. This might include things such as gender, other programmes your listeners have listened to within the platform and how many subscribers you have. This is useful if a lot of your listeners are using the platform.
- Allow you to create private podcast communities.
- Offer a website or blogging options for your show.
- Have a live podcasting option.
- Integrate with promotional tools such as Headliner, which creates media to market your podcast.
- Offer plugins so you can manage your podcast from your own website.
- Offer tools to analyse all this data and make comparisons between different episodes and look for trends and overall statistics.
- Some platforms also have a wing that enables dynamic ad insertion. Others allow you to buy ad campaigns or monetise your own podcast by taking ads for other programmes.
- Some platforms offer you premium levels of service or data for an extra fee. Do take time to understand these extras and whether you feel the additional benefits justify the increased spend. There's not a huge amount of variety between them in pricing.
- Some hosting platforms include automated transcription add-ons which can be useful in generating transcripts quickly for

your webpage, articles or search engine optimisation. Just make sure you check and correct them first: autotranscription software can make hilarious and not-so-hilarious mistakes. For accuracy, humans are generally more reliable.
- Some all-in one platforms go beyond basic hosting and even allow you to record multiple sources, add music and sounds and do some basic editing without the need for extra software.

One thing that's worth thinking about if you're seeking transparent and accurate data is to see if your chosen platform complies with the Internet Advertising Bureau's definitions for measuring statistics. You can find the podcast management technical guidelines here:

https://iabtechlab.com/standards/podcast-measurement-guidelines/

And if that's too much detail, here's a list of platforms that currently comply or are certified - but do check with yours for the latest updates.

https://iabtechlab.com/compliance-programs/compliant-companies/#

You are absolutely spoilt for choice when looking for a hosting platform. Alongside management and distribution some incorporate creation and monetisation options. Whatever is the biggest priority for you, you're bound to find several to match. Other than the services offered by each platform, the pricing scheme for platforms can also vary based on the amount of storage used, bandwidth or the number of downloads so will be another consideration for your pricing. Other than that, the look and feel of a platform and its output comes down to personal preference. Because the tech here is evolving, this is a competitive space and these companies are vying with one another to create the best experience for creators, innovating, listening to feedback, adding and enhancing features all the time.

To start your search, are a few well-known platforms you might want to compare:

Blubrry
Podbean
Simplecast
Buzzsprout
OmnyStudio

Soundcloud
Transistor
Castos
Captivate
Acast
Anchor
Megaphone
Libsyn
Art19
Audioboom
Spreaker

PRIVATE and PROTECTED RSS FEEDS

If you're making a podcast for private circulation – for example amongst your company employees - you likely don't want all and sundry to be able to access your content. In this circumstance you might have been previously reluctant to use a hosting platform, instead circulating via a cloud link or via an intranet page.

However, many hosting platforms now incorporate this option into their packages, generating individual, private RSS feeds so that you can control and monitor the number of people who hear your programme.

APPLE, SPOTIFY, GOOGLE AND AMAZON

In spite of the many options available, Apple podcasts is still the titan of listening platforms, and at the time of writing freely accessible. Additionally, a large number of listening platforms use Apple's database to power their own content. If you want to reach as many potential listeners as possible it would be a bit of an oversight not to put your programme on Apple podcasts. You'll need to do this by setting up an Apple ID (if you don't have one already) and logging in to Apple Podcasts Connect.

From there you can submit your RSS feed and keep an eye on progress. Allow a week in the schedule for your programme to be processed (it's usually faster). If there are errors, say in the size of the artwork, you will get a message to let you know. If this happens try amending this in your hosting platform, refreshing and then re-submitting.

https://podcastsconnect.apple.com

If you're asking someone else to do this for you, make sure you use a company ID or one that you can share access to if they happen to disappear into thin air or take a job at a rival company! Transferring ownership of a feed can be an unnecessary waste of your time.

From this platform you'll be able to glean Apple's aggregated analytics for users on the iOS11 Podcast app or later, or in iTunes 12.7 or later provided users have agreed to share their diagnostics. They also have listen-through rates which can be really useful in supporting the statistics you gather from your average hosting platform.

Spotify and Google Play are rapidly growing too, so if your hosting platform does not automatically do this on your behalf, submitting your programmes here can be done manually, as with Apple. Similarly you'll need an account to submit your programmes. Amazon have also begun to invite podcasters to distribute their content on Amazon, Amazon Music and Audible.

Some podcast hosts will give an option to submit your podcast to these platforms without the rigmarole of doing it yourself externally. It's worth checking whether this is done using your credentials in the RSS feed, rather than the host's, so that you can keep control over your feed wherever it goes.

Take a read of the agreement with each distributor before you sign up to make sure you're happy with the terms. Once again, in these platforms you can gather further data that helps inform a richer picture of your listeners and their habits.

https://podcasters.spotify.com

https://play.google.com/music/podcasts/portal

Once your podcast is live, you will want to share it in line with your marketing and social media plan. So let's take a deep breath, and get into that next!

PART 6 - YOUR CAMPAIGN AND STRATEGY

- **Integration**
- **What podcasting can add to your marketing mix**
- **Funnels and reservoirs**
- **10 top tips to supporting podcast growth**
- **Getting the team on board**
- **Making a great trailer**

This is where we bring your podcast programme and your strategy together.

As I may have mentioned already, your podcast and wider business goals should be aligned. Everything you do to market your podcast to your target audience should ultimately advertise and promote your business and product too.

In my opinion, this is the special sauce for making podcasts really get to work for your business. You can make a great programme in isolation. You can win awards for the intelligence, originality or acclaimed verve of your content. These things are worth the effort in many cases, but if you don't see an impact in how your customers engage with your business, an opportunity is lost.

If you win an audio or industry award it's going to bring kudos to the department and might even make a few nice press pieces. It might start the ball rolling in getting the word out to the wider world about your business and what you do. If you create a programme that has a few passionate followers, the passion can translate to your business. But if you don't get the reach in terms of listeners, your investment in this highly-engaged content channel won't achieve its full potential.

When businesses create programmes that dovetail with a wider strategy of digital engagement they are maximising their opportunities to reach different customers at different depths of a relationship. This means they can create awareness, attention, emotion, connection and importantly, build upon more transient interactions by providing value that compliments an existing experience. This is the rightful, future place of audio in business, now the podcast has matured.

A centralised digital team will be used to thinking of the company channels like different phone lines to different sub-sets of audiences. You don't necessarily get the same audiences on the same communications channels, nor are they always exclusive to one, and nor does that audience behave the same in each space, but every share of their attention is an opportunity.

As a with any sales funnel or - even if you're not selling something - an understanding of how these opportunities fit together and activate as a journey for your audience is vital. This will also spell out where you should be placing your podcast in this mix. Once you have this chain of anticipated behaviour in place you can design content around it, analyse the results and tweak things to get the best outcome - one that you can measure against your business goals.

If this sounds straightforward, that's because it really is, but if your business is caught up in the excitement of making a podcast it can forget about integration, especially if it becomes one department's pet project.

Podcasts make for a good investment if you build the correct funnel or audience journey around them, and crucially support and embed it across your organisation. People have talked about 360 advertising for decades now for a good reason - the more you deliver for your customers in terms of the things they see and consume from you on these channels, the more they will have a strong sense of what you're about, what you can do for them and why they should continue with you on the journey – that is – a positive reinforcement of their "purchase" habit. Even if you're not selling anything to your podcast audience, you are still bidding for their time and attention, which is your customer's most valuable commodity.

Here's the truth:

PODCASTS ARE FOR DEEP ENGAGEMENT

It's quality not quantity.
But you can get quantities of quality with the right approach!

According to RAJAR's MIDAS report from Spring 2020, 65% of people listen to the whole podcast episode. If that's a 30-minute long episode then that's a pretty amazing share of your listener's time.

Couple that with the fact that most people listen as a solo task and that's a very personal experience.

Buyers of radio will be used to enjoying the benefits of travelling with their listeners - from their breakfast tables, to school runs, to the office. Podcasts allow this to go to the next level - a self-selecting pool of headphone-listening, information-seeking individuals who have chosen your programme to meet their needs that day.

These two factors unique to podcasting - the impressively high listen-through rates and personal nature of listening - make podcasting a very powerful medium through which to convey messages and create feelings. It all adds up to trust and that all-important place in your audience's brain: Mental and emotional real-estate! Plus, it's proven that our memories work better where stories are involved, so if you want to share information that stays with someone, stories are the medium.

For this reason you'll want to manage your listener's expectations before they arrive at the decision to listen. Which we'll get to in just a moment.

But there are different kinds of media attention too, and this matters very much when designing your ideal audience journey.

It's sometimes useful to define content as 'lean-in' or 'lean-out', drawing a line between that which customers may absorb passively, in the background of other tasks, or incidentally in their day, versus that which they have actively selected or leaned-in towards, making (perhaps subconscious) decisions about their mood, feelings and needs in the process and making themselves receptive to whatever you choose to give them - in the hope that you deliver!

Setting expectations before the play button is pressed is important in being able to deliver the experience the listener is looking for. This is where the rest of your media content can play a role in developing that; setting up your listener, persuading them it's a good idea and rewarding them for giving you their valuable time when they make the leap.

Making your content discoverable can be a challenge when there is so much choice, so much quality and so much noise on podcast platforms, not to mention in the world beyond. Once you have someone's ear, quality content can do the work of keeping them.

Before we consider other advertising, it's worth just looking at the obvious easy targets, that is people who are already engaging positively with your brand or organisation on other channels. These are likely to be your most receptive first port of call.

A FUNNEL TO THE RESERVOIR

Where are you already in conversation with your customers and audience?

On your website?
On your social media?
On affiliate or fan social media?
At sites or in store?
In publications you distribute?
Via mailing lists?
Via events?
Via your products?
In public appearances or broadcasts?
In advertising?
In other podcasts?

Every touchpoint you have with your audience presents an opportunity to let them know about your podcast, and deepen an already existing relationship.

In all of these spaces you will be aiming to meet a need for them or will already have their attention. Even if they barely hover over your Instagram posts before scrolling on, you still have an opportunity to begin to raise awareness and point them into your podcast.

I'm talking here like the podcast is the ultimate destination for your listener, but only because your podcast is built to do other tasks (i.e. provide a rewarding experience for your audience, deepen engagement with your company and change the way they feel or behave in relation to your product or organisation).

Assuming that this is the case, your audience journeys might look something like the below. This also assumes that the further along the funnel, the fewer people you have engaging with the platform. This entails that the audience that does eventually make it to your podcast will be pretty committed to listening and will have clear expectations of what they'll get out of listening thanks to the filtering of your more widely-consumed and publicly available channels.

Obviously the funnel shape entails that not everyone on your social media platform will click the sharing link to listen to the podcast. Even fewer still will stay for the whole duration.

SOCIAL MEDIA > PODCAST
IN STORE / EVENT / WORD OF MOUTH > WEBSITE > PODCAST
MAILING LIST > LINK > PODCAST APP
BROADCAST > GOOGLE SEARCH > PODCAST

You get the idea, even if in reality, not all human behaviour is not so clean and linear!

That's why advertising across as many of these touchpoints as possible will add to the general awareness in a customer until that tipping point where they spill over into thinking something like: 'I've heard of that before, maybe I'll take a look'.

This seems pretty straightforward when you get used to thinking about your podcast as the goal in a chain of audience behaviour and not simply as an isolated, vibrant thing. This truly is something that can get neglected in the excitement of making a programme. Also, a podcast is by no means the end of your audience's journey, it's simply the start of a new and deeper relationship with you, so never losing sight of how you want your audience to behave, think and feel is crucial in keeping the thing alive and moving.

What's more, you'll likely have a plan of what you'd like that audience to do next, after they've become passionate fans of your podcast.

THE RESERVOIR

It's helpful to think of your regular, subscribed or returning podcast audiences as like a "reservoir" of your most engaged customers or potential customers. But I must also add that reservoirs, in spite of the often motionless appearance of their surfaces, are always in flux. They drain down when something else is hungry, and they fill up when the rains come. They harbour life, dog walkers, watersports and occasional unwanted algal blooms. They are ecosystems in themselves - albeit man-made ones. And if any of the environmental podcasts I've made can tell us anything, it's that no ecosystem exists in isolation.

Searching for patterns in the behaviour of living things is one of mankind's deepest preoccupations, manifested in the analytics and data junkie who constantly observes, learns and recalibrates communication strategy in line with each fresh new dataset, each fresh influx to the system.

I suppose what I'm trying to say with this analogy is that life will flow ever-changing through your audience funnel and the composition of your 'reservoir' will change over time, which is why the data and analytics will remain vital in providing insight into what your listeners need and keeping them engaged with you, your brand or organisation. There are always things to learn from data, so don't let preconceptions about your audience limit the way you create content. By all means have a theory and test it, but don't forget to adapt after the initial establishment phase! As you gather data and your volatile new audience becomes more established, you may learn things you did not anticipate about the kinds of people that want to listen to your content and perhaps even see new opportunities for your business.

Next, let's look at a list of best practice for ensuring your podcast can grow and continue to make the most of all the opportunities you have to engage with an audience.

THE CHECKLIST FOR SUPPORTING YOUR PODCAST GROWTH IN EVERY WAY

In short, art and inspiration are fundamental in making a beautiful piece of content, but to see it grow and reach people you need:

A multiplatform digital strategy with integrated funnels to service your audience.

That means....

Good, sticky content

This first and foremost: never forget the need for good content that identifies and serves its audience, aiming to solve a problem or create change for them. Use all your ingenuity to surprise, delight and addict. Now what about the other 80% of the work? Here are ten steps to giving it the best chance possible of being found by the right audience.

It's a tidy checklist but it belies the huge amount of work that actually goes into promoting a programme after you've made it. As a business you might want to bring in additional help, or your production company might also offer services to support this crucial part of the podcast process.

1. Great show notes, transcription and Search Engine Optimisation

The descriptions that you write for your podcast are more than the first few vital lines visible on your average podcast listening app. Did you know that these are available all over the web? By including links, backlinks and detailed information that's been optimised you can boost your visibility with online search engines. The web doesn't YET crawl audio as standard but by publishing transcripts of your show on your website you'll become even more discoverable by Google and the like. It also means that more people can enjoy your product in different forms, so if they're not big podcast listeners, you still have a useful product. Create a blog page on your website to market each episode and use the content for clips and soundbites that you can use in your social media marketing too. And don't forget to make sure your episode titles are also optimised to answer questions or topics that people might stick into search engines. The title plays a crucial role in helping someone decide whether to listen or not, for example, would you rather listen to"5 easy ways to create love in your relationship every day featuring celeb expert" or "Listening, dedication and respect with celeb expert"? Both of these titles have the interesting person featured and may both represent the content equally fairly, but one seems to offer a more immediate way to solve a problem in a positive manner.

2. **Trailers and appearances in other podcasts**

This can be a good way of advertising your show to audiences that have similar interests. It's a real-time "if you like this you might also enjoy" moment. You might want to approach the producers of a show direct to see if they'll embed one of your trailers or even have you on as a guest. You could arrange this as a 'swap' with the other podcast, effectively appearing on each other's shows in order to cross-pollinate the audience.

3. **Podcast and online advertising.**

Some platforms will distribute adverts for your programme in aligned categories to hit audience verticals for a cost. You can choose or be advised upon the correct audience category for your podcast, spreading impacts across a range of programmes that are also of interest. Bear in mind that costs can soar beyond what you paid for production of the series and even if they deliver the impacts, the distributor isn't responsible for how catchy your content is or whether the campaign actually delivers an increase in listens! You will probably be responsible for making the ad too, so make it catchy and intriguing with a clear personality and call to action, and showcase some of the best and most enticing clips from your show. Similarly there's nothing to stop you buying visual ads online which link through to listen to the show. The key thing here is to ensure they're delivered on platforms, websites and pages that already have a resonance with your intended audience and the people you would like to convert to your product. Some podcast apps also have in-app advertising which allows you to do this using a visual popup.

4. Work with Influencers for a reason.

There's a good reason to feature individuals with credibility and followings in your subject areas. By inviting contributions, sharing and commentary from the biggest talent in your sector you can hope to leverage their followings and help more people discover your amazingly useful podcast. Influencers are influencers often because they have a strong interest, expertise or passion for their subjects, and thus the right ones can not only alert passionate followers who care about the same things to your podcast, but they can help advocate for it and enhance the quality of your content too. If you already have well-informed public advocates for your organisation then why not ask them to review or share the podcast, if not appear on it.

5. Work with good Talent in general

This can have the same impact. Not only will you create a well-informed, quality programme thanks to the expertise of top guests and presenters, you might create something truly special by putting them together. By making something that just 'sticks' thanks to this special magic, your following will grow as a result of great content. In addition, asking your talent to share, promote and actively spread word about your programme will open you up to the people in their sphere that might also enjoy your show. Adding quality and credibility through the voices and people featured can leave your audience with strong feelings about your organisations. The grass-roots nature of podcasting means that anyone can self-publish, but a quality presenter who can form a consistent relationship with your listeners, create a unique tone, knows how to make their guests comfortable and is able to connect the dots for a cohesive narrative across the episode or series is so valuable. Likewise selectively showcasing the internal expertise and talent at your organisation can speak for the calibre, depth of knowledge and passion within.

6. Consider creating a skill for use on smart speakers.

It's a growing platform, and since Google made audio native in search, audio programmes available online are becoming more a part of our information-finding experience. If you regularly create short-form informative or news content you might find this a great way to embed yourself into a listener's routine, or to meet their needs. Definitely an area to keep an eye on.

7. Use every platform you have

Reach people across different media to let them know your podcast exists. Your audience may already be engaging with your organisation or business via TV, radio, print, books or other podcasts, but do they know they can find you in this space? Speak to them through your existing channels to let them know there is something of interest in their podcast app. Whether this is via advertising, articles, multiplatform broadcast content, special incentives or something else, by utilising these channels you might convert existing engagements into deeper, more passionate ones, and build an audience that doesn't just listen but advocates for you.

Press and PR can make a huge difference, especially if you can create something newsworthy that provokes conversation around the launch. Select and adapt the kind of content you share to the medium and audiences - give radio talk shows something they can discuss and give newspapers or magazines something that chimes with their audience. Pointing everyone to download and subscribe from the start can make a real event of things, but if you're spending money here, make sure you have something for people to listen to or you may be forgotten by the time your first episode lands! It's also worth releasing a few episodes at once when you launch, if you plan on a regular release. In this way you can give those who enjoy your show something to get stuck into and maybe even hooked on in the first instance.

Do you have an email list? Writing your press-releases and embedding links in here is a great way to catch already-engaged audiences who are already online. Just one tap and they can stream an embedded piece of audio, or by hitting your link the podcast opens in their app. You can now create links that allow you not only to program which app opens by device, thus increasing the chances they already have it on their phone, but which also allows you to track uptake by day. In the next section we'll talk about smartlinks.

You may in recent years have also noticed the odd billboard campaign for big name podcasts as you drive around. This is becoming more common as programmes are designed to be "appointment" entertainment, just like any on-demand TV show. And it looks pretty impressive too. In many cases the timeliness of your content will be ongoing, but it's the hook of your marketing that will create a sense of currency and new interest. This gives you the flexibility to time promotional campaigns that fit with the schedule of the wider business marketing agenda.

You may also have other platforms where you regularly talk to your audiences; perhaps a YouTube channel, a radio station, or TV station. If you are already talking to your audience in these places then it's a no-brainer that you tell them about your podcast here. Don't worry about losing users from one channel to the next, either. It's true that free-time is finite but people consume different media in different places. The depth and style of engagement is different, plus, podcasting can be enjoyed whilst doing other things AND it travels, even into those tricky no-4G zones. In my opinion, it makes sense to make yourself available to your audience in as many places as possible.

8. Social Media

This gets its own bullet point. Whether you live on Twitter, Instagram, TikTok, Facebook or some other app, you'll understand how your audiences on those platforms behave, interact and consume the stuff you offer up for them in different manners. Being primarily visual mediums, there's a chance to repackage juicy bits of podcast content into this language. If you've been savvy enough to engage a graphics team, or indeed film your podcast content, there is a world of creativity in how you catch the attention of these screen-scrollers. A few ideas for how you can create new content on social media stretch from the creation of captioned animations, to audiograms, which are clips of audio subtitled and given a visual treatment, video excerpts of the recording or maybe even additional 'behind the mic' promotional elements you've recorded with your guests and presenters. For this reason it makes sense to think about your strategy for social media promotion ahead of recording so that you can plan to get as much as possible out of your recording sessions and time with talent. Also, as mentioned before, make sure you request talent and guests share your podcast and podcast social media activity with their own audiences. In addition, if you are creating bespoke social media for your podcasts, make sure you follow, share and interact with similar titles and subject matter of interest to your audience. If your in-house team has found they have success with social media advertising, then listen to every piece of advice you can get and see if they'll work with you to implement it in a manner that's powerful to your audience.

9. Share your show with Apple.

There's debate about the exact percentage share per platform, but the majority of UK podcast listeners still use Apple Podcasts to listen.

Therefore, the scrollable banner (carousel) on Apple's 'Browse' tab is prime, prime real estate for helping podcast listeners discover your programme. Directly beneath that is the New and Noteworthy section that features releases that have caught the editorial team's ears. This is purely curated by Apple at their discretion and whether they choose to feature your work is up to them. However, if you don't tell them your programme exists, your chances of being spotted and getting on the billing are obviously decreased!

When you submit your podcast as a promo request to be reviewed by the editorial team, you will have the option to provide information about the nature of your programme, but also your plan for marketing, sharing and growth. This is where you will need to pitch the reason why your show should be featured, and where you can show your commitment to continuing to deliver excellent content.

Another good reason to have a solid pitch, reason and PR plan in place for the start. What change do you want to make for the audience? You answered this in chapter one.

10. Get reviewed.

Another powerful mode of discovery in podcasting is word of mouth. Or rather, recommendation from trusted sources. This might include writing to respected reviewers or potential fans with big, trusting audiences - online, in print, or on social - or reaching out to online communities, powerful review sites and mailing lists. Placing a comprehensive pitch document into the palms of powerful potential advocates, accompanied by an easy-to-listen link is a wise move. Just a quick Google of 'podcast reviews' will give you an insight into the many forums that exist online, but some will be more geared to your subject matter than others. Social media is good for this too - I sometimes have sitcom and drama accounts sharing my non-profit content on social media just because they're searching for it! Help them out by finding them first.

CONSULT YOUR TEAMS AND TAKE THEM ON THE RIDE

One thing that's truly essential Is to involve your own departments and teams and get them as excited about the podcast as you are. Even if you outsource the social media and additional content creation, it's down to your social media and digital teams to check, adjust and post these assets at the right time, frequency and manner for your audiences. You can brief external creators to give you amazing graphics and draft posts and blogs, but your own in-house teams work with your audiences every day. They understand their behaviour, preferences, interests and habits. They know how best to speak with them and how to interact effectively. For this reason it's worth including these people at the start of the planning process, taking on board their advice on when it is best to promote your podcast, and how you can ensure the podcast is aligned with all the bigger picture corporate messaging - for example when all the company channels are crammed with news from an industry event. By working together, you can get a picture of the hingepoints and opportunities in your audience's calendar and ensure that you share the right messages at the right time and in the right way.

I cannot emphasise enough the importance of aligning your audio activity with every other piece of advertising and marketing you and the rest of the organisation do. By consulting with different teams from the outset, you can bring together the goals of individual departments within a comms strategy and plan to avoid friction further down the line.

AVOID CHAOS AND OVERSPENDING: WORK OUT WORKFLOW

A big part of smooth, efficient and cost-effective productions are clean lines of communication. During production of your podcast and supporting assets, there may be several rounds of amendments or stakeholder feedback to incorporate. As with anything else in your business, how this will be delivered needs to be worked out from the start so that you can deliver feedback in an aggregated fashion. This means it can be actioned quickly and in one go. There's no use giving granular feedback to timecodes on different occasions as the edits will change the timecodes every time. You'd be surprised how many clients forget this and it creates quite a head-scratcher for the editor! Similarly, it is easier to adjust a script or paper edit than it is to adjust recorded and mixed audio, so incorporate the production process into your feedback workflow as advised.

As for your production company, in-house creators or suppliers, making sure they're clear on who to talk to about what and who has final signoff is also essential. You might prefer your producers to have a direct line to the on-mic contributors within your organisation but for the sake of clean communication and everyone's time, a project manner to act as a conduit within your business is a sensible idea. This individual can then liaise between departments and external suppliers, and can arrange working groups or regular meetings where all the stakeholders can get together.

This collaborative approach means that advice and questions are brokered to ease friction between departments and that ultimately team meetings can be a place to throw around ideas and propose experiments in a receptive atmosphere.

With so much detail, it's easy to forget the big picture, so as a reminder, the end goal of this cross-business collaboration is to make your audiences aware of a piece of audio content that they will find deeply useful or enjoyable. This will deepen your relationship with them as a business and benefit every department in turn.

HOW TO MAKE A GOOD TRAILER

There is a valid reason to have a good trailer for the launch of your podcast. This isn't just useful for advertising or pre-launch promotion.

When you set up your podcast feed you'll need to publish a piece of audio in order to distribute the RSS to platforms like Apple podcasts. Granted, you may not want this to be the grand appointment to listen that your first episodes are, but there is no harm in making sure it makes the programme sound exciting and entices a few early subscribers.

I made trailers on the radio for years and can tell you that this can be an art form in its own way. There are some very talented people behind the adverts and trailers you hear on the radio. There are also some deeply prosaic, common sense ones. And whereas you can't bottle creative genius in a how-do guide, it IS possible to list the essential components of a good trailer.

- Keep your call to action simple - listen on your podcast app / subscribe on your podcast app / search for podcast name. Whatever it is, pick one and make that the whole point. Whatever you do with your allotted time, your job is to convert your ideal listener into a subscriber, or at least spark their curiosity for the main programme.
- Creatively, you can do whatever you want. Just make sure it captures and holds the attention of the listener and provokes curiosity for the bigger programme. Get your presenters to record something new, write a short novel, or just feature the best clips of your show. As long as you catch the ear of your listener and convince them that it's going to 1) change their world 2) make their life better 3) improve their mood or 4) teach them something they don't know etc.
- Don't waste words. Brevity or "word economy" is an important broadcast skill, even if you don't have a word limit. In radio "Tight and bright" was the term I heard. If you say things simply, in the tone of your ideal audience, so you have more time for good creative and mucking around with sound design.
- Think of the clock ticking, and with every second that passes your listener's interest is more likely to move onto something else. Therefore get your message across whilst you have their attention.
- If all this feels like a strange new world to you then maybe employ a writer or producer.
- Here's a short checklist of the key elements for an effective trailer. How creatively you deploy them is entirely up to you!

- Attention-grabbing clips or sounds
- Identify the voice and why they're talking
- What's the question your programme explores, or what is the problem you're solving
- What your show delivers (in as concise a form as possible)
- Release date and call to action.

PART 7 - MEASURING SUCCESS

- **What data is available**
- **Measuring the effectiveness of marketing channels**
- **Measuring calls to action in your podcast**
- **When to make a change**
- **Assessing your campaign**

In the final part of this book we turn our attention to the all-important numbers. All-important, that is, if you have invested time and money and expect to see a return on these resources, or have to demonstrate this return to others in your organisation. Making audio is an enjoyable hobby, but as a business you need the hard data to prove it delivers value for you as well as your customers.

Working out the who, what, when, where, why and how of your podcast audience is the ultimate test of whether your investment has been worthwhile. The data available can help you make decisions about the audience, nature, style, distribution and frequency of your content and marketing. Knowing whether or not you've reached the people you wanted to reach and created the change you wanted is the reward for all your hard work, and it's one that never lies.

There is nowhere to hide in podcast stats. Interpreting them correctly on the other hand, is far more qualitative.

Before you made your programme, you established presumptions that informed the direction and style of the content you produced and may have incorporated these into a business plan. Now is the time to find out whether those assumptions were correct. Every set of data is going to enrich your understanding of this and ideally offer new ideas and questions to explore.

Let's start with what quantitative data you can gather.

THE NUMBERS

Most podcast hosting providers allow you to see:

Number of downloads (IAB compliant hosts will filter out repeat requests and display the number of downloads and streams). This is not a measure of how many people listen strictly, but how many people who intend to do so, as evidenced by their actively choosing to download the audio for now or later.

Location - Where in the world people are listening, with aggregate numbers by region.

Platform / Device - What sort of device or platform they were using to read the RSS feed, for example, Apple, Android etc.

Some podcast hosting providers allow you to see:

Listen-through data - the all-important test of how much time your audience will give your episode on average. This conversely also shows when you're a) failing to capture their interest or b) they simply have more important things to do.

App or platform - Which manner they were using to access your RSS feed and listen to the content.

And you can get more personal data, based on the consent users logged-in on a platform have given to share their behaviour. This data is always anonymised and aggregated though:

Also listened to...- This is interesting but be mindful that this will be based on the users within a certain platform and if that platform does comprise a large share of your audience, then it can skew your perception of your audience's tastes.

Age range - Always useful to pinpoint who your presenter's style and subject-matter is resonating with.

The trick to get right with analysing podcast numbers is to track them in all the different places you can. Using and IAB certified host will mean you can have an accurate idea of how many times that RSS feed is being triggered by unique devices. For example, you can use the analytics of your hosting platform, in addition to whatever you can glean directly from the Apple Podcasts Analytics interface. Once you've submitted your RSS feed to Apple Podcasts Connect, you'll be able to access analytics for your podcast for devices using software versions iOS 11, iTunes 12.7 or later, for example, and for users who have agreed to share this data for analytics.

If you read the user guide you will be able to understand how these data sets are gathered and gain a better understanding of what they are and are not telling you. You may not get the full picture but you can get a pretty decent one.

In addition, you might want to enter your RSS feed into a service such as Podtrac, to create measurement reports of your audience or set up audience surveys to gather a deeper, wider range of data from your most engaged listeners.

http://analytics.podtrac.com

THE BIG PICTURE

Ultimately, your podcast doesn't just exist to sound pretty. If it did, then you'd have deep pockets and be fully committed to doing brand-marketing for the long-haul. If you're a smaller business and perhaps using your programme for lead-generation, or to build interest, credibility or awareness around a certain topic, with a certain kind of person, then you want to understand their behaviour and habits to refine who you talk to and how.

So how to measure this?

SMARTURLS

It's likely existing audiences will hear about your podcast via your social media or other communication channels before they come across it in the wider realm, so ensuring you use trackable links to understand which channels are most successful can be helpful for this. A smartlink is a customised URL that can divert listeners to an episode, series or webpage of your choice. It's trackable and can make for an easier and friendly user experience.

Smartlinks can allow you to choose which app the content is automatically opened by depending on the device the user has and even where in the world they are. This is useful because it means you don't lose sceptical or first-time podcast listeners at the all-important stage where they think they have to download a brand-new app and learn how to use it. You can state that Apple users will open in the Apple Podcasts app, Android in Google Podcasts, Spotify, or whatever you like. Being able to divert people to the correct place for their country can also be useful if your content is localised.

You might have heard of Bit.ly and smartURL as platforms for creating smartURLs already. In addition, PodFollow.com is designed by podcasters who understand that the easier you make it for people to listen, the more they will listen! It also looks tidy on your social media as you can pick your handle and it's clearer to the passing user that it's a podcast, not a scary spam link, for example http://www.podfollow.com/enteryourpodcastnamehere.

IS THE PROMOTION WORKING?

You might be testing out the usefulness of different social media or online channels to funnel users into podcast listens. Using a bespoke smartURL for each platform, even for each post, will give you some granular data on how well your marketing works and what kind of posts are most effective. If you already have a clued-up social media team, those are the people best-placed to write content that catches the eye, but the call to action is crucial in being able to measure this. Don't just post 'search PODCAST TITLE' in your app. That is asking the user to stop what they're currently doing, open an app, look for the search function, type the title and wait patiently for the options to appear, before selecting the series that looks like the closest match. That is work for a tired brain, and I don't think people are on social media because they want to work, to be honest. Pairing your expertly written social content with a 'one click' smart link will make it as easy as possible for the viewer to hit a button and open the podcast app you have chosen for their device operating system, so make sure you use it!

It's harder to measure the impact of advertising upon your listener numbers unless you have included in that advertising a particular URL or offer code as your call to action. Normally an ad will push listeners to search for the programme in their favourite app. This means that the only way you can see its impact is 1) a statement of impressions delivered from the ad platform 2) an upsurge in listeners that coincides roughly with the period in which impressions were delivered.

If you don't get the latter, then you are just left with questions as to whether your ad was ineffective, or you were promoting to the wrong audience.

If you want to isolate the distinct impact of different organic funnels into your podcast, change the variables and test them one at a time, not all at once.

OFFER CODES, SURVEYS AND WEBSITES

If you want to understand whether the podcast does the job of converting listeners to further action, you need to be able to measure where they go afterwards. Depending on what you're trying to achieve, you might share a bespoke URL as part of your call to action, for example www.organisationwebsite.co.uk/podcastsearchterm. If you are hoping a customer will buy a specific product as a result of hearing about it in the podcast, you could give them a unique offer code or send them to a unique URL where they can get a discount. Don't forget to tell them how long it's valid for unless you plan on using it permanently.

If you have a really passionate audience, you might be able to persuade them to join a focus group or complete a survey to tell you more about themselves too. Simply having the presenter request feedback and sharing a form in the show notes can be a powerful way of gathering qualitative data that can inform future content decisions.

For those listening to players embedded on your website, it's easier to follow their behaviour within your own ecosystem. In addition to the benefits of looking like a professional organisation, maximising search engine optimisation and creating a home for extra and related content, you can look at what performs well here as a way of generating ideas for future content in the podcast.

THE WRONG KIND OF NUMBERS

If your analytics are showing you something you were not expecting, you have a few options.

First, bear in mind that growing and establishing a steady audience takes time and a good deal of marketing and promotion as already discussed. Your first series may not be the hit of the century but before you redesign your content, take a look at all the other ways in which you can support it. As mentioned before, the energy you put into marketing your precious vessel of content can make an enormous difference.

It would be a mistake to immediately blame the content for poor numbers, without asking how effectively the different elements of promotion have been activated.

If you have invested money in making this content and are disappointed that it's not number one in the charts remember that you have potentially created something that can exist and grow as it is discovered by a growing audience be discovered in perpetuity. Your content has the ability to become useful at any point you decide to promote it in line with the public or corporate news agenda.

What does it mean if you hired a celebrity to present it and expected the fans to flock, but they didn't?

Even the most well-established, quality digital organisations will ask themselves: what is a good number? A digital team used to thousands of interactions on their social media or website will still not know if they should be aiming for thousands or tens of thousands of listeners. At this point your own understanding of an existing audience will be helpful, but remember that you are also building a brand new one. Podcast listeners may also use social media and websites and listen to the radio and watch TV, but they don't listen to podcasts in the same way. Podcast listeners commit valuable time to topics - a lot of it. They give you their full attention in their homes, cars or workplaces. They devote personal time to this. Podcast listeners give unbridled access to their inner world, thoughts and consciousness. There is nothing more intimate than audio, nothing more honest. Don't expect people to come in the same numbers as do that eye-catching social post you can hover over, scrolling through the phone, whilst waiting for a friend. It really is about the quality of engagement you receive, rather than quantity, with this kind of content.

Having said that, lots of quality engagement is the ideal scenario, but it doesn't come overnight. If they flock easily to you with a celebrity presenter, they can flock away just as easily when you change presenters. Ultimately you want people to be valuing the words before they value who is saying it! Gaining the level of trust and commitment that podcast listeners give takes time, consistent quality and an unflinching instinct for what they want. It also takes a vast amount of support in terms of finding those people and convincing them to try the programme in the first place. Give it a little time to grow, before you give up and pivot to a different approach. There is a real difference between a dead-end and a slow start.

But if you've given it time, you feel you're really booming with your social media promotion, PR and marketing, leveraging all your brilliant guests and hosts and generally giving your target audience all they need to know there's a great podcast waiting for them, and you still aren't happy with the numbers or the kinds of interactions you're getting, this is the point you might consider revising your content. Hopefully you will at least have started to clean patterns in the data of what kind of content, marketing and title works for your audience and what doesn't. Even something as crude as download numbers can give you an insight into whether a particular marketing tactic worked, or the number of smarturl interactions can help measure whether you're promoting this on the right platform.

ANALYSIS AND REVIEW

Here are some useful questions to ask yourself and experiment with (although probably not all at once!). Like any good science experiment, identifying some clearly measurable variables and observing them first independently and then in conjunction will lead to the most accurate data. The number one goal of any such experiment is not to see the listener numbers go either up or down, but to learn something about what has driven that change.

- Am I using the right platform to promote this? Which platforms perform most effectively in terms of clicks and overall episode numbers?
- What sort of impact do I see by releasing social media posts or marketing content at different times and days?
- Do I see any impact when I tailor the episode subject matter to current news events? What about certain topic areas?

- How well are my web pages performing for each episode? How do these figures relate to their level of search engine optimisation for the topic?
- Which titles have the most or least downloads and what do these have in common? For example, do some seem to solve a problem or bring benefits to the lives of listeners more immediately on title alone? Is there a difference in the way they are written?
- Which guests and subjects are chiming with my audience? Is this what I would expect or want? How can I reposition this to shift the sorts of people who are tuning in to my content for the credible names?
- If listeners turning off before the programme has finished, what sort of content are they drifting in? Is this due to the average amount of time someone might have to spare, or is it more to do with a penchant for long, monotone interviews?
- Do I see growth in the listener numbers and do they seem to be gaining momentum? If not, have I supported this enough via marketing or is it time to shake things up?
- What surprising things have I learned about my podcast audience? Anything unexpected? How could this learning benefit the business?

STICK OR TWIST?

If you're creating a podcast, AND a podcast audience from scratch, patience and an analytical eye is the name of the game. Knowing when to stick or twist with you content and marketing strategy can be supported by watching the numbers, but you also need to give them space to grow and pass the point of volatility that most new, regular content will experience. If something isn't working, you have still learned something of value about your podcast audience. If you get a few surprises, that's all valuable information to support future strategy, and perhaps even to spark ideas of the sorts of content you use on your other digital platforms. Ultimately the data you gain over time will offer a wealth of insight, so even before you've tracked conversions, interactions or other behaviour, there is something of value to be gained in your statistics.

BEGINNING YOUR JOURNEY

It's my sincere hope that this book has not only inspired and informed you on how you could approach podcasts as a business, but also given you plenty of options to do this in a way that suits you. Most importantly, I hope you can also see the value that this exciting medium brings to deepening your engagement with a unique and bespoke audience, hopefully one that will be more inclined to become committed customers as a result.

There is no one way to market and deliver podcast content, just as there is no one correct way to market your business. The creativity and ever-evolving opportunities in the medium mean that the environment is an exciting one for any business to step into, and I hope these tools and approaches enable you to do this with greater clarity, confidence and effectiveness.

It's quite difficult to write broadly for a market that is so very diverse and so very much in flux, and to that end keeping a keen eye to the latest trends, fads, tech and ideas in this space is a must for any keen podcast publisher. The problems and limitations in podcasting today will be the opportunities that provide most possibility for growth in the future. As with any digital medium, its limitations are the thing that excites innovators in the tech space. We have seen enormous growth in the capability and sophistication of platforms to meet the needs of podcast creators and users in recent years, with the reward being a wider and wider uptake amongst populations worldwide, and a more serious place for the medium in gathering data that can truly refine business strategy and deepen our understanding of audiences.

The work you have done with this book will have guided you to consider which potential audiences you can build a relationship with through podcasting, and what topics you might choose to invite conversation upon. We've spent a lot of time thinking about your strategy and reflected upon how to analyse this data and adapt your content. We've explored how to market your podcast, in order to use your podcast for marketing! And I hope that you have become deeply excited thinking about the subject matter and manner in which you can entertain, inform and compel your audience. Whether or not you choose to work with an audio production company or start small, my hope is that some of the world of podcast production has been demystified so that you can approach this stage with confidence.

With any luck this guide will be a useful resource that you can dip back in and out of as you begin and continue your adventure in podcasting! Whilst this can be a deep and complex process with much cause for theory, reflection and analysis, you are now empowered and equipped to get out there and start building some amazing relationships with real people who, like you, are looking for a way to enhance their lives, connect with others, solve problems and better understand our world.

If you get stuck, there is a vibrant and exciting industry full of talented and imaginative producers from all sorts of backgrounds who will be all too passionate about helping you succeed in the wonderful world of audio. We'd love to hear your stories via podcastpioneers.com

Good luck!

Katharine Kerr, February 2021

ABOUT THE AUTHOR

Katharine Kerr is Director and Founder of Podcast Pioneers. After a career in network commercial radio production she left radio to pursue writing and journalism, but couldn't quite leave behind the incredible storytelling power of audio!

After successfully helping other production companies develop their branded audio content into award-winning programmes, she eventually turned a side-project into the business we now know as "Podcast Pioneers", uniting intelligent strategy with colourful, change-making audio storytelling.

For more information including blog articles please visit the website www.podcastpioneers.com

Press Information

Step-by-Step Podcasting For Business is a new book designed to help businesses get to grips with the world of audio marketing and communication.

In recent years, many UK business and organisations have embraced podcasts as an exciting and growing opportunity to connect with customers, audiences and individuals in depth.

This book aims to support those making the leap with a no-nonsense overview of planning, strategy and production, as well as guidance on how to market and experiment with your podcast content.

Whether the goal of the project is to educate, entertain or to shift perceptions, audio can be a powerful tool for businesses to incorporate into a wider communications strategy.

Author Katharine Kerr says it's never been more important for creators to speak from the heart:

"In turbulent times, discerning podcast listeners value quality programmes that connect them to our shared human experience. Original, surprising, gripping or delightful audio can be the remedy to our intense, screen-heavy world."

Step by Step Podcasting For Business guides the reader through the key questions each business should ask itself before launching a podcast. With a strong emphasis on strategic planning and clear goal-setting, the book guides businesses through the different tasks and insight required to kick-start a podcast campaign.

It also outlines some practical basics of production and recording, so that beginner podcast creators can explore options and feel empowered to hire in professional help or get hands-on in house.

"The human voice, sound and our imaginations the most powerful communication tools we have available. They allow us to connect with an individual's real decision-making engine: emotion"

For businesses just beginning their journey, as well as those who want to add strategy and insight to their output, this book aims to demystify the world of podcasts and help decision-makers confidently choose where to invest time and energy.

Find out more about the book and join the mailing list for updates via the Podcast Pioneers website, and follow @podcastpioneers on Twitter.

https://www.podcastpioneers.com/book

STEP-BY-STEP PODCASTING FOR BUSINESS

Publishing Disclaimer

Although the publisher and the author have made every effort to ensure that the information in this book was correct at press time and while this publication is designed to provide accurate information in regard to the subject matter covered, the publisher and the author assume no responsibility for errors, inaccuracies, omissions, or any other inconsistencies herein and hereby disclaim any liability to any party for any loss, damage, or disruption caused by errors or omissions, whether such errors or omissions result from negligence, accident, or any other cause.

The publisher and the author do not make any guarantee or other promise as to any results that may be obtained from using the content of this book. You should never make any investment decision without first consulting with your own financial advisor and conducting your own research and due diligence. To the maximum extent permitted by law, the publisher and the author disclaim any and all liability in the event any information, commentary, analysis, opinions, advice and/or recommendations contained in this book prove to be inaccurate, incomplete or unreliable, or result in any investment or other losses.